BOOKS BY KENNETH E. LONG

And They will Riot in the Streets -
A Nation Deceived is a Nation Enslaved

Macroeconomics -
Austrians vs. Keynesians

Introduction to Economics

Personal Finance -
Beware of Wolves in Sheep's Clothing

ECONOMIC ESSENTIALS
Theory and Application

Kenneth E. Long

Rose of Sharon Publishers

ECONOMIC ESSENTIALS -

Theory and Application

Copyright © 2021

Kenneth E. Long

ALL RIGHTS RESERVED. No part of this work covered by the copyright herein may be reproduced, transmitted, stored, or used in any form or by any means graphic, electronic, or mechanical, including but not limited to photocopying, recording, scanning, digitizing, taping, web distribution, information networks or information storage and retrieval systems, except as permitted under Section 107 or 108 of the 1976 United States Copyright Act, without the prior written consent from the publisher.

Rose of Sharon Publishers

roseofsharonpublishers@gmail.com

Cover Design

ISBN 13: 978-0-9963327-6-7 (paperback)

ISBN 13: 978-0-9963327-7-4 (ebook)

Printed in the United States of America

ACKNOWLEDGMENT

I am indebted to Steven Macon whose expertise in publishing would not have made this book possible.

CONTENTS

CHAPTER 1: TERMS ... 1

CHAPTER 2: GLOBALISM VS. NATIONALISM ... 19

CHAPTER 3: KEY PLAYERS ...37

CHAPTER 4: AUSTRIANS VS. KEYNESIANS ... 53

CHAPTER 5: GOVERNMENT OVERREACH ... 65

CHAPTER 6: FEDERAL RESERVE ... 87

CHAPTER 7: GOVERNMENT ... 103

CHAPTER 8: FISCAL POLICIES ... 115

CHAPTER 9: PRICES ... 125

CHAPTER 10: EMPLOYMENT ... 137

CHAPTER 11: TRADE & CURRENCY WARS ... 149

CHAPTER 12: DEPRESSIONS ... 165

ABOUT THE AUTHOR ... 189

Economist Norm Franz once stated:

"Gold is the money of kings, silver is the money of gentlemen, barter is the money of peasants —but debt is the money of slaves."

CHAPTER 1:
TERMS

SCARCITY

Scarcity means that there are not enough goods (something tangible) or services (something intangible) to meet consumers' wants and needs at a zero price. In a free market, the price mechanism decides who gets what and how much. A free good or service is a good or service whereby there is plenty for everyone who wants it at a zero price. Water from a public drinking fountain is an example of a free good.

THE ECONOMIC PROBLEM

The economic problem is that there is always scarcity, and resources are insufficient to satisfy our wants and needs. Therefore, we have to determine what to produce and how best to allocate land, labor, capital, and entrepreneurship. Economics studies this fundamental economic problem.

CHAPTER 1: TERMS

MACROECONOMICS

Macro means large; macroeconomics examines the economy in the large, such as unemployment, national income, growth rate, gross domestic product, inflation, and price levels. Macroeconomics focuses on the movement and trends in the economy as a whole.

MICROECONOMICS

Micro means small; microeconomics focuses on the decision-making process by people and firms. How do we make decisions to maximize our welfare? How does a business choose the best price and the best quantity to produce to maximize their profits or minimize their losses?

OPPORTUNITY COST

Economics forces us to make choices, and every decision entails an opportunity cost. Opportunity cost is that which you give up in the best alternative when making a decision. For example, when you attend a lecture—how much money are you giving up? If you could make ten dollars an hour and have three hours vested in the class, your opportunity cost is thirty dollars. Opportunity cost can be a pleasure you are giving up on the best choice. What would you rather be doing if you were not class? If you are giving up the joy of fishing, then that foregone pleasure is an opportunity cost. On a macro scale, we must make decisions, and every decision entails an opportunity cost.

CHAPTER 1: TERMS

MARGINAL ANALYSIS

You use marginal analysis each time you make a decision. The term margin means the last unit or the previous increment. Marginal benefit is the benefit from your previous action, and marginal cost is the cost of that last act. For example, imagine standing in front of a soda machine. How many dollar sodas will you purchase? To answer this question, economists always start with the first soda. Will you or will you not buy the first soda? You will buy the first soda if your marginal benefit is greater than your marginal cost. In other words, if you value the soda more than you value a dollar, you will exchange a dollar for a soda. Will you purchase a second soda? Yes, the answer is the same if you value the second soda more than you value a dollar. You will not buy a third soda if your marginal benefit is less than your marginal cost. Each time you make a decision, you go through this same thought process.

LEVERAGE

Suppose you need to move a thousand-pound rock, what would you do? You would place a smaller rock next to it and put a long pole on the small rock and under the big rock. The longer the bar, the easier it will be to move the big rock. In so doing, you are using the pole as leverage to move the rock. Some people use borrowed money as leverage to buy stock, which economists call purchasing stock on the margin. You can buy, let's say, $1,000 worth of stock by investing $500 of your own money and borrowing the rest from your stockbroker. However, when the stock price falls, your losses are magnified. When a company has

CHAPTER 1: TERMS

more debt than equity, economists say that it is "highly leveraged."

PRICE ELASTICITY OF DEMAND

Price elasticity of demand is a measure of a consumer's responsiveness to a change in price. When a price change has a small effect on the quantity demanded, demand is inelastic. If a good faces an inelastic demand curve, a price increase will increase total revenue; the money gained exceeds the money lost. The demand for a good is elastic when a price change will affect the quantity demanded. With an elastic demand curve, a price increase will reduce total revenue; money lost exceeds money gained.

MORAL HAZARD

A moral hazard occurs when someone pursues an activity without regard to potential losses because there is no penalty for the loss or failure. For example, a banker is willing to make risky investments because he believes the government will cover his losses. You may be careful when making decisions if you know you will bear the consequences of a wrong decision, but you will tend to take more risks if you know that someone else will pay the cost of your wrong decision.

RENT-SEEKING

Rent-seeking occurs when people seek a bigger slice of the economic pie rather than make the pie bigger; rent-seekers

CHAPTER 1: TERMS

make money without producing more goods or services. Whether legal or illegal, rent-seekers impose economic costs.

STOCK VS. FLOW

What effect will a national minimum wage law have on the economy? The answer depends on your point of view. One line of reasoning supports a national wage standard because higher wages will increase consumer demand, increase production, and more jobs. This line of reasoning is looking at a national minimum wage as a stock variable. A stock variable measures something at a particular point in time. At times economists will use the terms "static" and "dynamic" instead of the words "stock" and "flow" to describe these events.

If people can earn higher wages, everything else being equal, consumer demand will increase. But can we assume that nothing else will change when the government imposes a minimum wage on the nation? What effect will this government-imposed mandate have on businesses? Will this mandate increase costs for business? And if so, what impact will these higher costs have on employment?

A flow variable is a variable over an interval of time. If variable A changes, variable B might change, which might affect C, etc. When Congress makes decisions to do this or that, there is a tendency for politicians to look at things as a stock situation and not consider the flow. For example, politicians tend to believe that a ten percent tax increase will increase government revenue by ten percent. But this approach to decision-making ignores dynamic analysis. Dynamic analysis recognizes that

CHAPTER 1: TERMS

when taxes increase by ten percent, consumption and investments are affected.

ECONOMIES OF SCALE

Economies of scale recognize that as the scale of operation increases for a business, its costs decrease over the long run, time in which a firm can change its plant capacity. A larger size typically allows a firm to take on more specialized machines. It can take advantage of skilled labor, which contributes to lower costs as productivity increases. The increase in efficiency allows a firm to lower its price to increase its total sales. For example, a farmer who owns a small farm may not purchase an expensive modern tractor. A farmer who owns a big farm can justify buying a large, expensive tractor (more efficient) because of the large volume.

By forcing smaller competitors to raise their wages, larger firms are put in a favorable position because they can afford the high salaries due to its economies of scale. The small competitor may not afford the higher wage because of its higher costs. By driving smaller competitors out of the market, larger firms can increase their market share. Large corporations have an incentive to engage in rent-seeking in hopes of convincing politicians in Washington DC to raise the minimum wage.

DERIVATIVES MARKET

Derivatives are contracts between parties; they are speculations on some future event. The value of a derivative is reliant upon or derived from an underlying asset or group of

CHAPTER 1: TERMS

assets. In other words, the value of a derivative is derived from the value of something else. The most common underlying assets for derivatives are stocks, bonds, commodities, currencies, interest rates, and market indexes. Derivative contracts are a part of the "futures" market because the results will take place in the future. Two parties can bet on anything, such as the price of a stock, the price of an agricultural product, exchange rates on the international market, or anything else. The derivative market is the largest market in the world.

Let's say you and I make a bet that it will rain or the sun will shine on some future date, for example, May 5. We wager one hundred dollars, and we draw up a contract and both sign it. I bet that the sun will shine, and you bet that it will rain that day. If the sun shines, you own me one hundred dollars, if it rains, I owe you one hundred dollars. This contract now has a value of one hundred dollars to whomever is on the winning side of the bet. Now let's say that you want out of the contract. You can sell you're your part of the contract to someone else. They will pay you whatever the two of you agree upon.

HEDGE FUND

Hedge funds are alternative investments using pooled funds that employ different strategies to earn active returns for their investors. A hedge fund is a pooled investment fund that trades in relatively liquid assets and is able to make extensive use of more complex trading, and risk management techniques in an attempt to improve performance. A liquid asset is an asset that can easily be converted into cash within a short amount of time.

CHAPTER 1: TERMS

MARGIN CALL

Buying stock on the margin means that a person buys stock with borrowed money. A margin call occurs when the value of an investor's margin account falls below the broker's required amount. An investor's margin account contains securities bought with borrowed money (typically a combination of the investor's own money and money borrowed from the investor's broker). A margin call refers specifically to a broker's demand that an investor deposit additional money or securities into the account so that it is brought up to the minimum value, known as the maintenance margin. A margin call is usually an indicator that one or more of the securities held in the margin account has decreased in value. When a margin call occurs, the investor must choose to either deposit more money in the account or sell some of the assets held in their account. When Bill Hwang's hedge fund Archegos defaulted on a margin call he was forced to sell $30 billion in stock to satisfy the call.

HEGEMONY

Hegemony refers to the dominance by either a social group or a country over others. The dominance may either be economic, political, or military. The term originated from the Greek word "hegemon" meaning "leader" or simply "dominance over." Hegemony is the position of being the strongest and most powerful and therefore able to control others.

CHAPTER 1: TERMS

FEDERAL RESERVE

The Federal Reserve is America's central bank. President Woodrow Wilson, and Congress gave up control over the nation's money supply when it transferred authority from the government to the world private banking cabal with the Federal Reserve Act of 1913. A cartel of eight families owns the Federal Reserve and other central banks around the world. They are Goldman Sachs of New York, Rockefeller Brothers of New York, Rothschild Banks of London and Berlin, Lazard Brothers of Paris, Israel Moses Sieff Banks of Italy, Kuhn and Loeb and Company of Germany and New York, and the Warburg Bank of Hamburg and Amsterdam. The Federal Reserve is listed in the telephone book's white pages, while the US Treasury is listed in the yellow pages. Fed employees' email address ends in .org, not .gov.

Commercial banks can multiply money, but only central banks can create money. Before the banking system can multiply money, someone has to make a deposit. But the Federal Reserve does not need a deposit; it can create money by merely pushing a few keys on its computer to credit a client's account by X amount. All currencies are debt instruments; they are floating abstractions that profit the world's bankers. At the top of a dollar bill is printed "Federal Reserve Note." A note is an IOU; it is an agreement to pay interest to the note owner, the Federal Reserve. Dollars come into existence when the government sells bonds to the Federal Reserve. The Bureau of Engraving and Printing of the government converts a small fraction of this borrowed money into physical dollars.

CHAPTER 1: TERMS

QUANTITATIVE EASING

Quantitative easing (QE) is a form of unconventional monetary policy in which a central bank purchases longer-term securities from the open market in order to increase the money supply and encourage lending and investment. Buying these securities adds new money to the economy, and also serves to lower interest rates by bidding up fixed-income securities. It also expands the central bank's balance sheet.

MODERN MONETARY THEORY

Modern Monetary Theory (MMT) is a big departure from conventional economic theory. It proposes governments that control their own currency can spend freely, as they can always create more money to pay off debts in their own currency. The theory suggests government spending can grow the economy to its full capacity, enrich the private sector, eliminate unemployment, and finance major programs such as universal healthcare, free college tuition, and green energy. If the spending generates a government deficit, this isn't a problem either. The government's deficit is, by definition, the money we owe to ourselves. Keynesian economists tend to support this MMT, while Austrians see it as inflationary and a ticking time bomb that will eventually destroy the economy.

CANTILLON EFFECT

Artificially low interest rates tend to channel money to the safest, most credit worthy, and/or favored borrowers, which are seldom the best job creators. Economists call this the

CHAPTER 1: TERMS

Cantillion Effect. In our modern economy, the Cantillon Effect is at play with a stratified socioeconomic impact, favoring investors over wage-earners. Cantillon's original thesis outlines how rising prices affect different sectors at different times and suggests that time difference effectively acts as a taxing mechanism. Modern Monetary Theory (easy money policies) favors investors over wage earners because the monied class has preference in the loanable funds market, the market where people lend and borrow money, and wage earners get the dregs. The artificially low-interest rates favor the rich over the poor, the asset class over the wage earner. The Cantillon Effect illustrates how the uneven distribution of wealth in society grows ever more uneven with low-interest rates. While the low-interest rates favor investors, the average income person receives less interest income on their savings.

THUCYDIDES TRAP

When an emerging power threatens to displace an existing power, there is a tendency toward conflict and sometimes war. When the existing power relies on its military and its political influence instead of competing economically with the rising power, the emerging power ultimately gains dominance over the current regime. A characteristic of a Thucydides Trap is when the declining power is guilty of hubris. Hubris was a character flaw often seen in the heroes of classical Greek tragedy, including Oedipus and Achilles. The familiar old saying Pride goeth before a fall" is talking about hubris. Hubris describes a personality quality of extreme or foolish pride or dangerous overconfidence, often in combination with arrogance

CHAPTER 1: TERMS

and the over extension of resources. When the art of diplomacy between powers declines, when the declining power relies on brute force, this indicates that we are in a Thucydides Trap.

FALSE FLAGS

A false flag concocts a crisis, stirs a reaction, then proposes a solution that will convince people to support a policy that they would otherwise not support. Perpetrators of false flags are masters of deception. A false flag event will stir emotions and will be followed by a news blitz. Shortly after, authorities will identify a scapegoat with little or no concrete facts to back up the accusation. The higher the shock value, the more spectacular the event, the more people killed, or claimed killed, the more severe the unemployment and bankruptcies, the fewer people will question the authenticity of the occurrence. The term comes from the old days of wooden ships when a ship would hang the flag of its enemy before attacking one of its own—then it would blame the enemy for the attack and thereby gain public support.

STOVEPIPING AND GASLIGHTING

Stovepiping is similar to false flags. Whereas a false flag uses an incident to convince people to take action, stovepiping uses incorrect information to sway public opinion. Gaslighting sows seeds of doubt in a person or a group, hoping to make them question their memory or cherished beliefs. The term "Gaslighting" comes from a 1938 play by Patrick Hamilton. Throughout the play, the abusive husband, Gregory, manipulates Paula to make her believe she has gone mad. He leads her to

CHAPTER 1: TERMS

think she's stealing things without realizing it and hearing noises that are not there. Gaslighting hides truths from the victim—thus, the perpetrators of gaslighting seek power and control.

ESG

ESG stands for Environmental, Social, and Governance, and refers to the three key factors when measuring the sustainability and ethical impact of an investment in a business or company. Most socially responsible investors check companies out using ESG criteria to screen investments. The relationship between ESG and the board of directors of companies is still being defined. Discussions around the "G" (i.e., governance) are often spearheaded by the nominating and governance committee with involvement from the full board— particularly when assessing how these risks integrate with the enterprise risk management (ERM) program or impact long-term strategy. ESG became mainstream in 2020. Using ESG metrics is an extended version of Marxist Critical Race Theory—scoring, reshaping, and mastering the financial world using Marxist tactics.

THE GREAT RESET

COVID-19 could destroy the economy and lead to the birth of a new system. The World Economic Forum (https://www.weforum.org) and the book COVID-19: THE GREAT RESET by Klaus Schwab and Thierry Malleret assure us that the modern world after the pandemic will be better, more inclusive, more equitable, and more respectful of Mother Nature

CHAPTER 1: TERMS

once we reset the present social/economic system and replace it with a new and better one.

Chapter 2 of the book shows how past epidemics have altered society and how COVID-19 can do the same today, and that germ phobia will reshape society. Chapter 4 calls for a restructuring of the world's economy and a global government. A sub category of the World Economic Forum is the Centre for the Fourth Industrial Revolution where societies and personal lives are highlighted. In their conclusion, on page 243, they ask the question: Could COVID-19 have the force to ignite profound changes?"

According to the World Economic Forum, COVID-19 will usher in the Great Reset, which will be imposed by violent shocks like conflicts and even revolutions. The Forum is an avenue for the world elite to put us in bondage and debt by eliminating private property, the free enterprise system, installing fake democracy by stamping out real democracy, controlling the media with their propaganda, and replacing Judeo-Christian western values with paganism.

We can't grow the economy without growing the debt, and debt is the very thing that will bring down the economy. An increase in debt Economist Norm Franz once stated, "Gold is the money of kings, silver is the money of gentlemen, barter is the money of peasants—but debt is the money of slaves."

The Great Reset is a coordinated plan that has been years in the making before the virus; it is a fresh coat of lipstick on an old pig; it is a social and economic world transformation. The Great Reset will centralize power in fewer hands through Orwellian surveillance technologies. Yuval Noah Harari wrote an

CHAPTER 1: TERMS

article for the Financial Times titled The World After the Coronavirus. The opening sentence reads This storm will pass. But the choices we make now could change our lives for years to come...they will shape not just our health care systems but also our economy, politics, and culture" Technology has made it possible for the government to monitor us and punish anyone who dare break the rules.

HEGELIAN DIALECTIC

"Hegel's dialectics" refers to the dialectical method of argument employed by the 19th Century German philosopher Georg Wilhelm Friedrich Hegel, which relies on a contradictory process between opposing sides. The Hegelian dialectic is a framework for guiding our thoughts and actions that lead us to a pre-determined solution to a problem. If we do not understand how the Hegelian dialectic shapes our perceptions of the world, then we can become victims of the perpetrators who wish to control our thoughts and actions—unwittingly, we help to implement the pre-determined outcome which ultimately leads to our bondage.

BLACK SWAN EVENTS

The term Black Swan originates from the belief that there are only white swans. However, the opinion changed after a Dutch explorer discovered black swans in Australia—people consider low probability but high impact occurrences as black swan events. Nine-eleven, the threat of global warming, and COVID-19 policies are black swan events.

CHAPTER 1: TERMS

RED HERRING EVENTS

A red herring event is an event that leads people to wrong conclusions by constructing a false narrative.

CRITICAL RACE THEORY

Critical race theory (CRT) is a movement based on the premise that race is not natural but a socially constructed (culturally invented) category that perpetrators use to oppress and exploit people of color. Critical Race Theory is a Marxist framework that views society only through the lens of race-based oppression.

Critical race theory is opposed to traditional values. There was a time when a country identified itself by ancestry and common ethnic nationality. Not so for America. If America abandons its political and economic structures, it will lose its identity more thoroughly than a country defined by a common ethnic and cultural background. The fabric of America's identity are the institutions of personal liberty, free contracts, jury trials, uncensored news media, regular and free elections, open competition, private property rights, religious freedom, and habeas corpus.

WOKE MOVEMENT AND CANCEL CULTURE

Woke is a term that originated in the United States, referring to a perceived awareness of issues that concern social justice and racial justice. It is like saying we have to wake people up from their preconceived notions of race, particularly white

CHAPTER 1: TERMS

privilege, but it can also include anything contrary to the official narrative. Cancel culture is a modern form of ostracism in which someone is thrust out of social or professional circles, whether it be online, on social media, or in person. Those who are subject to this ostracism are said to have been "cancelled."

According to a new mathematics teaching resource guide, Math is embedded with white supremacy culture that must be rooted out by the social justice police and consequently transformed to fit their teaching protocols. Oregon's Department of Education approved the controversial teacher's resource titled, A Pathway to Equitable Math Instruction. The 82-page manual is not a math curriculum but rather a toolkit for teachers designed to influence the climate of education by helping teachers identify ways where white supremacy culture shows up in teaching mathematics to students in grades 6-8.

Following are examples of the Woke Movement and the Cancel Culture. Angela Davis is a left-wing activist who has been deeply involved in Communist politics, feminism movements, and other radical causes. Although Butler University scheduled her to be the lead speaker at a Joint Struggle and Collective Liberation event, the university canceled her appearance because she supported Palestinians. When Georgia passed a bill requiring voters to provide photo identification when they vote, Major League Baseball announced moving the All-Star Game from Atlanta to Denver, Colorado. United Airlines has abandoned merit-based hiring practices to appeal to the Woke Movement by notifying that fifty percent of pilot trainees will be women and minorities. The US government has threatened to boycott the 2022 Beijing Olympics over China's Uighur Muslims' treatment.

CHAPTER 1: TERMS

The Cancel culture has convinced the Cleveland Indians baseball team to change their name after 100 years.

CHAPTER 2:
GLOBALISM vs NATIONALISM

Globalism stands for the stateless state made up of floating and interchangeable parts everywhere and nowhere at once. Globalism is a network of central banks, international, political, and monetary institutions like the United Nations, the International Monetary Fund (IMF), the World Bank, and the European Union. Globalists believe in collectivism, where the government will coerce people to conform to the will of the state. Nationalists believe in individualism, where there is freedom of personal choice within a democratic republic. People still work together collectively under the rule of law, but their interaction is voluntary. Whereas the Globalists want to break down national boundaries, Nationalists favor strong borders between countries. Left-leaning people tend to be globalists, and nationalists tend to be on the political right. The Globalists believe in restructuring the global network of trade, communication, immigration and transportation of national and regional economies. The term includes such topics as culture, media, technology, politics, and biology. Many of the world's

CHAPTER 2: GLOBALISM vs NATIONALISM

central bankers are Globalists. The story of how the central bankers gained control of the world starts with Mayer Rothschild (1744-1812). Driven by the desire for money and power, the central bankers have masterminded many wars since the 1800s to finance both sides of the conflict between nations. Four of Mayer's five sons had sons of their own and decedents manage banking centers around the world.

MULTICULTURALISM

America has been multi-ethnic but not multicultural. A multi-ethnic society accepts people from all cultures but expects them to live and adhere to the general beliefs and customs of the host nation and contribute to the welfare of the country. Unfortunately, globalist ideas have transformed Europe from multi-ethnic to multicultural, and America is heading in the same direction. Like Constantinople and Lebanon in earlier times, multicultural societies risk losing their cultural and ethnic identity. When professional football players refuse to stand during the national anthem playing, they are demonstrating their support for multicultural policies over multi-ethnic policies.

Multiculturalism says that society should be tolerant of all cultures and that one country's beliefs are no better or worse than any other nation or group of people. Multiculturalism provides for an economic exchange with no assumed national mission and no particular people for whom the country exists. Multiculturalism says that this space belongs to everyone and therefore to no one in particular. Multiculturalism is married to the concept of Globalism. Multiculturalists believe in cultural relativism. Cultural relativism believes that all beliefs, customs, and ethics relate to the individual within his social context. In

CHAPTER 2: GLOBALISM vs NATIONALISM

other words, "right" and "wrong" are culture-specific. What people consider moral in one society may be immoral in another culture. Since no universal standard of morality exists, no one has the right to judge another society's beliefs and customs. Multiculturalists believe in the equality of outcome where everyone should end up in the same place; they do not believe in the equality of opportunity. If inequality is the system's fault, something unjust has happened, the system has oppressed someone, so the society should protect and uplift perceived disadvantaged groups and discriminate against perceived advantaged groups.

Inequality of outcome is why multiculturalists discriminate against straight white males and Christians while non-white, homosexuals, heterosexuals, transgender people, women, and Muslims are considered victims. The University of Michigan held a two-day seminar teaching employees how to deal with their "whiteness." The university plans to spend $85 million to increase campus diversity while paying its chief diversity officer $385,000 per year. Some universities require their students to take diversity courses as a requirement for graduation. For example, the University of Vermont has hosted retreats where the university teaches white students to believe that differences in group outcomes are due to the privileges granted to white males. In addition, a reporter for Texas State University newspaper, the University Star, had an article published titled "Your White DNA is an Abomination."

Multiculturalism lambasts white privilege, demands social justice, and advocates safe spaces where people can evade criticism or unpleasant ideas. Multiculturalists discourage using certain trigger words, sometimes called negative feeling words, that might offend or make someone or a group feel

CHAPTER 2: GLOBALISM vs NATIONALISM

uncomfortable. Multiculturalists believe that the government should pass equality laws to achieve social justice. For every unprivileged group, there is a privileged group. Globalists wail against the uneven distribution of wealth but suppress any reference to communism because Western capitalistic societies accept the profit motive. Milton Friedman, a famous economist of the Chicago school of thought, often stated: *"any society that puts equality ahead of freedom will end up with neither equality nor freedom, and any society that puts freedom ahead of equality will end up with both freedom and greater equality."*

We are in a world struggle between Nationalism and Globalism, between Collectivism and Individualism. The Globalists embrace multiculturalism, whereby society should be tolerant of all cultures because one country's beliefs are no better or worse than other nations. This shift to globalism has led to hate speech laws enabling the government to punish citizens for speaking their minds. Any opinion that differs from the globalist dogma is considered hate speech. Laws that divide groups against groups, persons against persons, males against females undermine society's freedom of speech. When people are intimidated from speaking their minds, freedom of expression flies out the window. The term racist comes loaded with negative connotations. It suggests that there is something evil, wrong, or immoral about a perceived favored group, such as white males of European heritage standing up for their beliefs. Multiculturalists use the term as a form of oppression, a weapon of social control that encourages one group to subordinate their interests to the interests of other groups under the threat of being accused of a hate crime.

Buzzfeed, a leading digital media company valued at $1.5 billion, published an article blaming white people for ruining

CHAPTER 2: GLOBALISM vs NATIONALISM

America. The Root, an online media company, owned by Univision with about 8 million visitors a month, has published several articles accusing white privilege of many sins. Because multiculturalists assert that white people have historically dominated other groups, society must suppress white people to equalize the different groups. In other words, multiculturalists believe that racism against white people can solve the problem of racism.

HATE SPEECH LAWS & CENSORSHIP

Canada's anti-Islamophobic laws allow the government to punish citizens for speaking out against multiculturalist policies. Any opinion that differs from the globalist dogma is considered hate speech, and a person can receive up to two years in prison for violating hate speech laws. Canada's hate speech laws cover any public communication that promotes hatred by gender identity or gender expression. These laws make it illegal to use the wrong gender pronouns when addressing people, and guilty persons can be fined and forced to attend anti-bias training programs. There is no universal agreement on what constitutes hate speech, and therefore interpretation is left to the ruling authority in each case. When two Roman Catholic bishops in Venezuela prayed that God would deliver Venezuela from government corruption, the government instructed prosecutors to investigate them for a hate crime. The Venezuelan government has used hate crimes as an excuse to abandon any pretense of democracy and human rights.

You can choose your gender identity in New York City. However, authorities can fine you up to $250,000 for failure to use and recognize employees, tenants, customers, or client's

CHAPTER 2: GLOBALISM vs NATIONALISM

preferred names, pronouns, and titles regardless of what sex the person was at birth. You can find a list of pronouns for New York City from a list of 31 politically correct different genders, one for each day of the month! The Commission on Human Rights defines gender identity as *"The internal, deeply held sense of one's gender as male, female, or something else entirely."*

Google and Facebook accounted for the majority of digital advertising outside of China. The dominance of this duopoly influences how people receive their news. The trend is for people to encounter news articles via search engines and social media. The most popular sites are Facebook, YouTube (owned by Google), Twitter (a partner to Google), and Facebook's Instagram. Facebook promotes content shared by friends and family that encourages interaction between people and de-emphasizes news media content. Facebook determines which content is allowed by judging which posts are meaningful interactions among users. Facebook claims that If you do not have meaningful interactions, we will de-emphasize you. Only Facebook can determine what is and is not significant interaction. This practice means that publishers like BuzzFeed, who publish social and lifestyle content, qualify for preferential treatment over news publishers. This stance by Facebook is similar to that of Google, which discriminates against low-quality content.

German lawmakers have passed a law whereby Facebook, Twitter, and other social media companies could face fines of up to 50 million euros ($57 million) if they fail to remove hate speech within 24 hours. Social networks also have to publish a report every six months detailing how many complaints they received and how they dealt with them. German police have raided people's homes over social media posts that allegedly

CHAPTER 2: GLOBALISM vs NATIONALISM

contained hateful content. The European Council approved a set of proposals that would require web companies to block any hate speech videos. The problem with these laws is that they fail to provide sufficient safeguards for freedom of expression.

YouTube has developed a spell check for what it considers hate speech and algorithms to filter the news. Viewpoints contrary to their own, the government, or their largest advertisers are discouraged. Consequently, it has removed advertising in some YouTube programs, a practice called demonetization, and it has delisted others. For example, YouTube has delisted a popular news program, RT (Russia Today). Advertisers do not want their brands to consider objectionable content and take offense if their advertising money supports the videos' creators. In addition, Facebook has partnered with Politifact and Snopes to mark what they consider false information, lowering offenders prominence in the news feed. This shift in news prioritization would be Facebook's most aggressive attempt yet to rein in what it considers fake news. This censorship by the tech giants, Facebook, Google, YouTube, and Twitter is unnecessary if the reason is to protect them from lawsuits, at least in the United States. However, this discrimination is not legal protection because Section 230 of the 1996 Communications Decency Act grants interactive computer services total immunity for their users' content. Therefore, the tech giants have no liability resulting from anything that their users post or tweet.

Google and Facebook's advertising policies can harm the alternative news media. Twitter has refused sponsored tweets from immigration opponents. Twitter, Microsoft, and Google have signed a private censorship agreement with the European Union to halt the Conservative Movement's rise in France and

CHAPTER 2: GLOBALISM vs NATIONALISM

Germany. This censorship of the Tech Titans is a new phenomenon. When 600 to 700 migrant men molested girls in Cologne, Germany, in one of the worst violent riots since World War Two on New Year's Eve 2016, the following day, the police chief said it was an uneventful night and a relaxed evening.

The Globalists' belief in rectifying any injustice has led to the Canadian government of Ontario passing Bill 89, "Supporting Children, Youth and Families Act, 2017." This act gives the government the legal right to remove children from families that refuse to accept their child's chosen "gender identity." The bill states that a parent's failure to recognize and support a child's gender self-identification is a form of child abuse. A child in these circumstances should be removed from the situation and placed into protection. California used the system to correct a perceived injustice when it became the first state to allow its residents to opt for a gender-neutral designation on birth certificates, recognizing a third, non-binary gender category for Californians. The latter do not identify as either male or female.

THE WAR AGAINST FREE SPEECH

The Universal Declaration on Human Rights was proclaimed by the United Nations General Assembly in 1948, and the UN adopted the International Covenant on Civil and Political Rights in 1966. Both declarations guaranteed the right to freedom of expression. Article 19 states that *"Everyone shall have the right to hold opinions without interference and everyone shall have the right to freedom of expression."* Freedom of expression is essential to every human right. Both declarations proclaim that *"everyone has the right to freedom of opinion and expression; this right includes freedom to hold opinions without*

CHAPTER 2: GLOBALISM vs NATIONALISM

interference and to seek, receive and impart information through any media and regardless of frontiers."

Despite these provisions, the European Union has declared war on free speech when opinions are contrary to cultural relativism. Cultural relativists believe that all cultures are worthy in their own right and are of equal value. Even for those with conflicting moral beliefs, purists do not consider the diversity of cultures right and wrong or good and evil. Globalism in Western Europe has led to a loss of national purpose and identity in most countries. Europe is on its cultural deathbed, and Canada's multicultural policies that promote diversity are pushing it down the same path. Canada is an example of a country moving toward a system of values instead of national identity because there has been an erasure of culture, ethnicity, and European heritage imposed on society from the top down.

DIVERSITY

The Merriam-Webster dictionary defines diversity as *"the condition of having or being composed of differing elements, especially the inclusion of different types of people (such as people of different races or culture) in a group or organization."* However, the Globalists have redefined the term to mean the inclusion of individuals representing more than one national origin, color, religion, socioeconomic group, and sexual orientation.

Marquette is a Jesuit University in Milwaukee. In 2014, a student of Marquette criticized an ethics professor for telling a student he could not criticize the practice of same-sex marriage in her class because that would be homophobic. Multiculturalism

CHAPTER 2: GLOBALISM vs NATIONALISM

does not allow criticism on issues that are offensive to a protected group by limiting diversity. When another professor defended the student and refused to apologize for his defense, the university fired him. A Wisconsin court backed the university's decision. The Wisconsin Institute of Liberty and Law claims the firing violates his contract, which promises professors freedom from threats or dismissal over constitutional rights, such as free speech.

Teaching the classics has become an anomaly on many college campuses. For example, Seattle University students held a week-long sit-in to protest the classical emphasis in the humanities college. The sit-in led to the dean's departure after a student complained that they are teaching us the only thing from dead white dudes. Students at Oregon Reed College staged a protest claiming that too many courses were caucasoid, eurocentric, and oppressive. Yale's English Department changed its curriculum after 150 students signed a petition demanding a change. As a result, it is now possible to get an English degree from Yale without studying Chaucer, Shakespeare, or Milton.

A group of white individuals of different ethnic groups who speak other languages and have different customs is not diverse; it is not multicultural. According to this definition, people living in a homogenous, nationalist, Christian white country are not distinct enough, regardless of individual differences. Globalists label such a group as exophobic (tending to discriminate against different groups), homophobic (having negative attitudes against lesbian, gay, bisexual, and transgender people), anti-Semitic, and racist.

Globalists portray diversity as a concept that promotes moral values and furthers equal dignity and goodwill. They use

CHAPTER 2: GLOBALISM vs NATIONALISM

the idea as a bludgeon against white cultures to convince them of the need to show more compassion for disadvantaged groups of non-white and non-traditional people. How can one turn a blind eye to the suffering of others? The lie of the Globalists is that diversity can enhance livelihood, but in reality, it can spawn conflict. It can destroy social cohesion, as witnessed by the growing occurrences of riots in much of Europe. The concept of diversity is in direct opposition to nationalism.

The Merriam-Webster Dictionary defines diversity as the condition of having or being composed of differing elements, especially the inclusion of different types of people (such as people of other races or cultures) in a group or organization. However, the Globalists have redefined the term to mean individuals representing more than one national origin, color, religion, socioeconomic group, and sexual orientation. In other words, a group of white individuals of different ethnic groups who speak different languages and have different customs is not diverse; it is not multicultural. According to this definition, people living in a homogenous, nationalist, Christian white country are not mixed, regardless of individual differences. Globalists label such a group as exophobic (tending to discriminate against different groups), homophobic (having negative attitudes against lesbian, gay, bisexual, and transgender people), anti-Semitic, and racist.

Diversity does not include differences of political opinions because diversity can only mean thinking multi-culturally or like a Globalists. Globalists do not want people to have different thoughts; they want everyone to believe as they do; thus, Globalists favor censorship. Globalists use diversity as a weapon against Nationalists. Globalists use minority groups to further their agenda; they use minority groups as a wedge that

CHAPTER 2: GLOBALISM vs NATIONALISM

breaks apart the cohesion of the white majority group. Globalists portray diversity as a concept that promotes moral values and furthers equal dignity and goodwill. Globalists, Multinationals use the idea as a bludgeon against white cultures to convince them of the need to show more compassion for disadvantaged groups of non-white people. How can one turn a blind eye to the suffering of others?! The lie of the Globalists is that diversity can enhance livelihood, but in reality, it can destroy the culture by destroying social cohesion. If enhancing diversity made a country strong, it would encourage social cohesion, but it only spawns conflict.

MULTICULTURALISM LEADS TO ETHNOCIDE

Ethnocide is the deliberate destruction of members of a national, ethnic, racial, or religious group. In this time of history, the culture is Western civilization. Ethnocide is the reason for the destruction or removal from public view of historical statues. Statues that symbolize an ethnic culture, which some people construe as prejudice and racists, should be banned. Because the white race has dominated others, symbols of the white race are considered evil. Multiculturalism is the separation of nation and state. Multiculturalism views a country not as a vehicle to advance and protect the interests or values of a specific group. Instead, it provides for an economic exchange with no assumed national mission and no particular people for whom the country exists. Multiculturalism says that this space belongs to everyone and therefore to no one in particular.

The multicultural model departs from the traditional view as a nation-state whereby the state or government exists to serve its nation or people. For example, Sweden protected its people,

CHAPTER 2: GLOBALISM vs NATIONALISM

its language, culture, and traditions stemming from their Western Civilization roots. The state protected Swedish values and interests. Lawmakers have since transformed Sweden from being multi-ethnic to being multicultural—favoring no particular people. Consequently, Sweden has committed ethnocide whereby there is no default or identity of what it means to be Swedish. The Swedish people do not exist whereby they can claim to be Swedish separate from other people. Foreigners have just as much claim to Sweden as people as the Swedish.

There is no wisdom in a people who fail to protect their culture, customs, and way of life. Why is there no wisdom? Because in secular societies, there is no God. Liberals, Globalists, tend to believe that people are born good, and therefore God need not play a role. Conservatives, Nationalists tend to think that people are not born good. People are not born evil, but human nature is not always good, and therefore since people are not inherently good, we need God's wisdom to show us the way.

Secularism is good for the government but bad for society; the more extensive the government—the smaller the individual. If people are not going to be accountable to God, they will put their faith in government if they do not trust God. It is not the government that has made people good in America; Biblical teachings have made good people—wisdom begins with the fear of God. The secular world has brilliance and knowledge—but there is no wisdom. Spiritual strength is necessary to have moral strength—democratic and cultural values are not enough to save people from forces bent on destroying them. In a secular society, everything has to be watered down because of offenses—including the truth. Pope John Paul II called Europe, where secularism reigns supreme, the

CHAPTER 2: GLOBALISM vs NATIONALISM

culture of death. A multi-ethnic society accepts people from all cultures but expects them to live and adhere to the general beliefs and customs of the host nation and contribute to the welfare of the country. A multi-ethnic society expects immigrants to integrate into the host country. Globalist ideas have transformed Europe from being multi-ethnic to multicultural and are at risk of ethnocide, of losing its cultural and ethnic identity. Christianity is facing elimination in its Biblical homeland.

CULTURAL MARXISM

The emphasis on equality of outcome is rooted in Marxist ideology and the Communist Manifesto, where Karl Marx saw history as a struggle between oppressors and the oppressed. Globalists and multiculturalists believe that Marx failed because of his emphasis on economics, so they have taken Marxism from pure economics and married it to culture. Inequality exists because powerful social groups have oppressed weaker groups, so the system should correct this imbalance.

Marxism explains the power struggle between different wealth groups (poor, middle-class, wealthy, bourgeoisie, proletariat, etc.). Cultural Marxism describes a power struggle between different identity groups or cultures(women, men, gay, straight, black, white). Europeans, Canadians, and Americans have embraced the idea of cultural Marxism, and as such, they tend to be multicultural but not multiethnic. They believe that people are all the same and all have equal value, and cultural diversity will positively affect their nation. The Globalist notion that man is good contradicts the Christian teachings that man needs God's guidance through his Word to be good.

CHAPTER 2: GLOBALISM vs NATIONALISM

A good read on the subject of Europe is *The Strange Death of Europe, Immigration, Identity, Islam* by Douglas Murray. Murray states: "*Europe today has little desire to reproduce itself, fight for itself or even take its own side in an argument.*" Murray believes that the people of Europe have given up on protecting their traditions and that diversity is sweeping away their culture. This lack of identity has made Europe ill-prepared to defend itself from the onslaught foreigners.

EUROPEAN UNION

The European Commission of the European Union is not elected, but it is accountable to the European Parliament, and the Council of Ministers represents all the EU member states. The European Parliament is only an advisory body to the EU Commission made up of people who have sworn their loyalty to the general interest of the EU. The Globalists who control the EU believe that the enemy is the nation-state, but they fail to understand that dangerous ideologues have caused world wars, and they are ideologues.

The European Union is an anti-democratic institution. The globalists who control the EU believe that the enemy is the nation-state, but they fail to understand that dangerous ideologues have caused world wars, and they are ideologues. The European Union does not represent European values, such as freedom of expression, the right to self-determination, the concept of the nation state, and the idea of democracy. The European Parliament is only an advisory body to the EU Commission, a small group of unelected officials who have sworn their loyalty to the general interest of the EU as a whole more than to the interests of their respective countries.

CHAPTER 2: GLOBALISM vs NATIONALISM

The EU does not accept ideas contrary to its own by stressing multiculturalism and diversity over nationalism and self-determination; it is an ideological entity opposed to alternative viewpoints. The EU's leadership believes that the EU is good. Anyone who disagrees with their policies is xenophobists, Islamophobists, sexists, or fascists influenced by fake news, propaganda, and hate speech. The EU supports the idea of free speech, but they believe that the opinions of intolerant people should not be allowed. Or, in other words, the EU is against free speech. The leadership of the EU is composed of radical people with grandiose ideas of a world utopia, a one-world government. Political correctness laws have made European governments and Canada ineffective in asserting national values, the rule of law, and women's rights.

Europe's culture, heritage, and traditions are under attack. In the spirit of globalism, Sweden has accepted more immigrants per capita than any other country. In 2016, Sweden proclaimed itself to be a humanitarian superpower. Since then, the nation's head law enforcement officer has stated that the police can no longer uphold Swedish law, and he has requested help from the populace while areas of the country have reverted to Islamic rule. Meanwhile, many law enforcement officers in Sweden are quitting their jobs. Immigration can be good for a country. America has been a success as the world's melting pot because its cultural diversity made it vibrant because migrants contributed to the nation's economy, and the number of immigrants was not so large as to destroy the country's identity. However, because Sweden has violated these guidelines, the Swedes could be a minority in their own country by 2040. The Swedes have discouraged immigrants from adopting Swedish traditions, and many Swedes even deny that there is such a thing as a Swedish

CHAPTER 2: GLOBALISM vs NATIONALISM

identity. The Swedes consider themselves to be citizens of the world, and they believe that people of the world are all the same and all have equal value.

Why have the Swedes exchanged peace and prosperity for fear and inequality? Firstly, peace and prosperity have been the norm for so long that the Swedes take their shared beliefs and goals for granted. Secondly, many Swedes have abandoned organized religion. As a result, they have lost their moral compass, or if they are Christians, they believe that it is the Christian thing to do to help all less fortunate people and convert them to Christianity if possible.

The two world wars have influenced events in Europe. European countries tend to blame the wars on extreme nationalism. Adolph Hitler wanted to establish a living space for the German people. So, Europe has overreacted and embraced globalism as an alternative to nationalism. Sweden closed its borders to Jews during World War II, so out of guilt and as an act of repentance, it has opened its borders to immigrants who, in their minds, are fleeing persecution and war. Unfortunately, Europe's welfare state has made its citizens dependent on the government, and it has become a pot of honey for militant migrants representing a full-blown invasion force.

The welfare state is dependent on a high level of taxation, and excessive taxation is dependent on a compliant and supportive population. The contract between the people and the welfare state was that everyone maintains the system, and the system gives back to meet society's needs. This system works if the people have shared customs, beliefs, and history, but the plan fails with too many takers and not enough givers. Instead of

CHAPTER 2: GLOBALISM vs NATIONALISM

Europe expecting immigrants to conform to European ways, Europe has conformed to the ways of the foreigners.

CHAPTER 3:
KEY PLAYERS

BLOCKCHAIN & 5G NETWORK

You can view the different cryptocurrencies in different rooms. You can be in the Bitcoin room with other people using Bitcoin, or you can be in the Ethereum room with everyone using Ethereum. The blockchain is the basis of cryptocurrencies like Bitcoin and Ethereum. The blockchain is a shared, immutable ledger for recording the history of transactions. Unlike national currencies that monetary authorities can bring into existence willy-nilly, there is a limit to the units of cryptocurrencies that can come into existence at any point in time. The danger to our freedom is when a central authority controls the currency and brings us all into the same virtual room. In this case, if we fail to cooperate with central demands, the foremost authority can prevent us from buying and selling anything. In that case, we will have relinquished our freedom and become wards of the state. With cryptocurrencies, there is no central control. A cryptocurrency is a virtual currency secured by cryptography where individuals store records in a virtual database. National currencies have a centralized platform, like the Federal Reserve. Cryptocurrencies use servers and hard drives to trace each

CHAPTER 3: KEY PLAYERS

transaction. There are close to 1,400 cryptocurrencies in the world, and many have versions of blockchain technology.

The blockchain is so efficient that corporations like Walmart are experimenting with the technology. For example, it used to take Walmart a week to trace the origin of a piece of fruit. The blockchain method can find the same information in a couple of seconds. Corporate spending on blockchain software is in the several billions of dollars a year.

The 5G network uses more bandwidth than previous versions, but more towers are needed to transmit the radio waves. The advantage of 5G is that it is much faster than the 4G network and can keep billions of devices connected in the cloud without compromising speed. Smart cities are attracting private investors to help build the infrastructure needed to bring them into the wireless 5G world. Europe, China, and Russia further down this 5G network, with the United States trailing behind. The 5G network will eventually revolutionize the world by digitizing communication, robotics, and new technologies like self-driving cars. Deployment of 5G wireless Wi-Fi internet service is gaining speed. The potential health risks from the proliferation of new cellular antenna sites are a concern, but not enough to deter this new technology.

DEEP STATE & NEW WORLD ORDER

We can all end up in a blockchain–5G network digital prison. In the future, the system will digitize you. You will be able to walk into a store, pick what you want off the shelves, scan it with a wireless handheld scanner or smartphone app, and walk out with the network recording every purchase. Kroger,

CHAPTER 3: KEY PLAYERS

Amazon, and Walmart, are already using this technology. In the future, it will be possible that naysayers of the establishment, the New World Order, will be made persona non grata without the ability to buy or sell. So the question is, who will control the levers of power?

As the size of the federal government grew during the 1800s, politicians adopted the practice of meritocracy whereby the civil service could not lose their jobs for political reasons to maintain continuity from one administration to the next. Nevertheless, there are unelected groups of people of the civil service, the deep state, who have a plan and act to put limits on presidential power. Problems arise when the ambitions of civil servants exceed the parameters of their jobs.

The term Deep State was originally used by Peter Dale Scott back in the 1950's. In his writings, he described the deep state as a parallel system to the public system, inside and outside the federal government. In his book, *The American Deep State: Wall Street, Big Oil, and the Attack on U.S. Democracy*, last published in 2014, Scott defines the deep state as people who have the resources to shape the direction of the world. Mike Lofgren spent twenty-eight years working in Congress, his last sixteen years as a senior analyst on the House and Senate Budget Committees. In his book, *The Deep State - the Fall of the Constitution and the Rise of a Shadow Government,* he gives an insider's explanation of who runs Washington regardless of which party is in power. People of the Deep State govern the United States with limited input from the President, Congress or citizens. According to Lofgren, the overhauling of the civil service must be the cornerstone to fix a broken government.

CHAPTER 3: KEY PLAYERS

According to Kevin Shipp, a former CIA officer, and an anti-terrorism specialist, there is a difference between the Shadow and Deep states. According to Shipp, the Shadow Government is on top of the pyramid, and the Central Intelligence Agency (CIA) is the central node. The Deep State and the Shadow Government are two different entities in a vast trillion-dollar matrix that influence government policy. The Shadow Government rules over the Deep State under a shadow of secrecy, fear, and intimidation. The Deep State is a massive multi-trillion dollar entity that includes the military-industrial complex. Both the Shadow Government and the Deep State try to manipulate the federal government from behind the scenes with the news media's help. Money, power, and greed connect the Deep State and the Shadow Government.

The New World Order aims to forge a one-world government promoting the centralization of power, which is also the goal of the modern-day Progressives and Globalists. The New World Order means different things to different people. A one-world government based on the concepts of personal freedom, a bill of rights, and individualism would be a good thing. But the one-world government discussed in this book is very different. The New World Order of the United Nations intends to control all people and resources with a world federation, a world parliament, a world court, a global police force, and a universal monetary system. The New World Order supports the concept of globalism over nationalism, collectivism over individualism, and autocracy, which is a society structured from the top down instead of the bottom up.

People will be willing to give up their freedom if they feel threatened by an external enemy. The New World Order combines the political, military, economic, scientific, cultural,

CHAPTER 3: KEY PLAYERS

and religious aspects of society like the cords of a rope. Each strand is composed of people in the outer layers who may be clueless about the central goals. The ultimate goal is to promote one leader who will rule the world. The New World Order influences the mainline news media because only if enough people are ignorant of its purpose can it succeed.

The book *Report from Iron Mountain*, 1967, is about the New World Order. In 1963, government insiders met underground in New York State at Iron Mountain to devise a strategy for social cohesion. The existence of an accepted external menace, then, is essential to social cohesiveness as well as the acceptance of political authority." War has always been a rallying force as the foundation of an expansive government. People will seek security, give up their independence, and support an ever-larger government if they feel threatened by an external enemy. The report suggests that a credible substitute for war is a menacing social enemy like gross pollution of the planet and global warming. If human activity is a threat, then the government must control human activity. The book claims that fictitious alternate enemies must be found for social control of the population if a transition to peace is ever to come about without social disintegration. The authors advocate blood games for the management of aggressive impulses. The movie *Hunger Games* illustrates these blood games. The specifics, the how to control human activity, are presented in the United Nations Agenda 21 and Agenda 2030 discussed later in this book. Presently, 37 cities on five continents are participating in The Rockefeller Foundation's 100 Resilient Cities group. These cities can receive grants from the Rockefeller Foundation, and it is the first step for the Foundation to implement central world control.

CHAPTER 3: KEY PLAYERS

CENTRAL BANKING

Banking is central to world dominance. The Swiss Federal Institute of Technology did a study to map the power structure of the global economy. The gist of the research is that there is a Super-Entity of 144 corporate fronts, with 75% of these fronts being financial institutions named the One Bank, which controls 40% of the global economy and all the big banks in the world. The world economy is estimated to be about $70 trillion, so 40% of this is $28 trillion, which is ten trillion dollars larger than the United States' GDP. The Swiss research did not say that this One Bank owns 40% of the global economy. It claims that this entity controls 40% of the world's economy. In a society where the rule of law protects the everyday person, there would be a check on this global power in a system where the average person can claim ownership. But we no longer live in societies where the average person can claim ownership. Because most people are in debt, they do not own their house or car; the lender maintains control. COVID-19 magnified this process.

Societies need a hierarchy to maintain order; the first entity is the central bank and not the federal government. As proof, we only need to consider the Federal Reserve. Despite calls from Congress to audit the Fed, the Fed has refused to open its books to anyone. Private bankers control our money supply, not governments. Violating agreements to gain an advantage over other members is always a problem. Unless there is some way to coerce the members to cooperate, eventually, someone will cheat. The solution to cheating is for the members to partner with their respective governments and pass the cartel agreement into law. The government gains because it can hide behind the central bank. This partnership happened in the US with the passage of the Federal Reserve Act of 1913. This arrangement benefits the

CHAPTER 3: KEY PLAYERS

central bankers because it puts the central bank in a position to write the rules. The government can no longer create money, but it must borrow from the central bank; the Fed then monetizes the debt and charges the federal government interest. The taxpayer always pays via higher taxes and/or inflation.

Because cash is an obstacle to the New World Order, its goal is to establish a universal virtual currency. People can only buy and sell digitally where money is bits and bytes on a computer in a cashless society. India has declared that 90% of its paper money will no longer be legal tender. The European central bank has stated that it will stop printing high-valued notes. Denmark is the first country to ban cash, and Venezuela outlawed almost half of its currency. Canada and Singapore have phased out their large denomination bills, and the Philippines, Denmark, and others are nudging citizens to electronic payments. If official virtual currencies replace cash, whoever controls your bank account, controls your life. In a cashless society, the government can track and record all your financial transactions. Transgression against the government, real or imaginary, could mean that your life would be over until you made good. When you buy a cup of coffee, the government knows how many you drink and from where you drank it.

THE TECHNOCRATS

The New World Order embraces the beliefs of technocracy, which is the science of using technology to transform society into harmony with nature. A great read on the subject is *Technocracy Rising - The Trojan Horse of Global Transformation, 2015-16*, by Patrick M. Wood.

CHAPTER 3: KEY PLAYERS

The New World Order turns Christianity on its head. It was Aldous Huxley in his book *Brave New World*, 1932, who predicted that society would end in a scientific dictatorship where unelected officials, technocrats, would rule. The New World Order has a plan to unite the United States, Canada, and Mexico into one cohesive unit where the leaders are appointed and not elected. Technocrats would merge countries into regional organizations and then combine the regional bodies into a one world government. The New World Order turns Christianity on its head; it puts nature over man whereas God of the Bible puts makes man supreme.

NEOCONSERVATIVES

The "Neocons" believe that it is our willingness and our military power that makes America great. Neoconservatives advocate the use of force and manipulation to attain goals. Neocons are people involved in the secret manipulation or control of government policy and have no regard for the democratically elected leadership. They may or may not be government officials.

The Project for the New American Century (PNAC) was a neoconservative think tank (1997-2006) that had strong ties to the American Enterprise Institute. In a PNAC's policy document *Rebuilding America's Defenses*, the group calls for total military world domination. Many PNAC members held high-level positions in the George W. Bush administration. Many Republicans have begun to question the old neocon foreign policies that dominated Bush's GOP despite the fact that we are still involved in neoconservative wars.

CHAPTER 3: KEY PLAYERS

Since the early 1950s, the Neoconservatives have led the United States in foreign exploits resulting in regime changes. However, neoconservative influence in America and the world has waned. Wesley Clark rose to four-star general and was named director for strategic plans and policy of the Joint Chiefs of Staff. As Supreme Allied Commander and Commander in Chief of the U.S. European Command, Clark knew that neocons in the military were plotting to overthrow the seven middle eastern countries of Iraq, Syria, Lebanon, Libya, Somalia, Sudan, and Iran.

A Neoconservative does not have specific goals other than to have a predominant influence over world events and to control the world's resources. The word hegemony means leadership, a predominance over other people and nations. Hegemony occurs when people believe that America holds a special place globally and that America should rule over others.

Paul Craig Roberts was the United States Assistant Secretary of the Treasury for Economic Policy in the Reagan administration. In his book, *The Neoconservative Threat to World Order: America's Perilous War for Hegemony*, he explains on page one that the Soviet collapse in 1991 gave rise to the neoconservative doctrine of U.S. world hegemony. According to Roberts, the neoconservative doctrine defines the United States as an indispensable, exceptional country above all others. Neoconservatives believe that this superiority gives it immunity from international law. Therefore, the first objective of U.S. foreign and military policy is to prevent the emergence of a new rival. Senator Marco Rubio, a neoconservative, stated in his maiden Senate speech that America remains a watchman on the wall of world freedom.

CHAPTER 3: KEY PLAYERS

President Ronald Reagan stood against world leaders, but he was not a neoconservative. He threatened the Soviet Union when it tried to put atomic weapons in Cuba, and he intervened militarily in Grenada, Lebanon, and Libya, but his operations were temporary. He did not have a goal to dominate countries over the long term. According to Roberts, when the Neocons became too forceful, Reagan drove them off.

Most people believe that the United States has a history of spreading democracy and good faith worldwide. However, this may not always be true. In his book *Overthrow* (2006), Stephen Kinzer chronicles America's hegemony over countries starting with Hawaii and ending with Iraq. Most Americans do not realize that Hawaii was an independent country before the United States overthrew its monarchy in 1893. Kinzer chronicles fourteen countries in which the U.S. toppled sovereign nations and often replaced the democratically elected heads of state with a dictator who agreed to do their bidding. *The Brothers*, another book by Kinzer, is about John Foster Dulles and Allen Dulles. During the cold war of the 1950s, the brothers were most responsible for America's hegemony described in *Overthrow*.

Kinzer writes about Mohammed Mossadegh, who was Iran's first democratically elected Prime Minister in 1951. He was educated in America, loved everything American, and tried to westernize Iran. In 1952, his picture was on the cover of *Time Magazine* when *Time* proclaimed him as the man of the year. At the time, England controlled oil and railroads and kept the majority of the profits, leaving Iran with a pittance. When Mossadegh tried to negotiate a better deal, England, with the help of America's CIA, sent Kermit Roosevelt, the grandson of President Theodore Roosevelt, to overthrow Mossadegh by way of lies, bribes, and deceit. The coup was successful in restoring

CHAPTER 3: KEY PLAYERS

the Shah to power. The Shah ruled with an iron fist while acquiescing to Britain's demands until 1979, when Grand Ayatollah Khomeini overthrew him in an Islamic revolution. According to Kinzer, if we had given Iran a better deal, Mossadegh would have stayed in power, and there would have never been an Islamic revolution. Instead, this neoconservative technique of peacefully overthrowing world leaders and replacing them with men of their choosing was so successful that the CIA repeated this scenario in other countries.

In his 2004 book, *The Confessions of an Economic Hit Man*, John Perkins explains the how the CIA used hit men to gain control over other nations. According to Perkins, the CIA would hire private companies, such as Chas. T. Main, to send trained personnel into countries disguised as economic experts to convince them to take out loans to fund construction and engineering projects that would supposedly lead to economic growth and prosperity. The scenarios presented by these hit men were overly ambitious, and many of their projects were not economically feasible, thus causing loan defaults and loss of property.

The International Monetary Fund (IMF), the sister organization of the World Bank, would broker deals with these bankrupt countries. Now the U.S. government (the CIA), with the help of the World Bank, could extract concessions. For example, instead of paying its debts, a country could give up its mineral rights, or agree to help the United States with its vote in the United Nations. The country could also relinquish its revenue from the country's airports, parking fees, etc.

The objective of the loans was to force countries so far into debt that they would not be able to meet their obligations to

CHAPTER 3: KEY PLAYERS

the IMF. When nations cannot pay their debts, the IMF forces them to cut spending on retirement benefits and other social programs as austerity measures. The money saved by the austerity measures goes to the central bankers. Without a compromise between creditors and the IMF, indebted countries are likely to continue to face demands for painful retrenchment with little reward. Since China and Russia established the Asian Infrastructure Investment Bank in 2017, America's influence over other countries will wane.

According to Perkins, there is a three-pronged approach to taking over a country. The first is to send in hit men. If they fail, the second phase is to send in jackals who are professional assassins, and if they fail, the government engage the military. In *The New Confessions of an Economic Hit Man*, Perkins explains how the jackals have come home to the United States—in the form of bankers, lobbyists, corporate executives, all eager to lure Americans ever deeper into debt.

PROGRESSIVES and LIBERALS

People who focus on using government money for social programs are Liberals. People who focus on making institutional changes to meet specific social objectives are Progressives. A Progressive would not be satisfied with funding programs without changing the rules of the game. For example, instead of funding health care, progressive politicians passed a new Patient Protection and Affordable Care Act (Obamacare) in 2010 that transformed the American economy's one-sixth. When Congress passed the act, it was 906 pages; by 2012, it had grown to more than 20,000 pages. The Obamacare law would be 7 feet tall if stacked one page upon another.

CHAPTER 3: KEY PLAYERS

Some economists believe that lengthy and convoluted laws like Obamacare that no one will read and no one can understand are examples of the Cloward-Piven strategy. The Cloward-Piven process is progressive, started in 1966 by American sociologists and political activists Richard Cloward and Frances Piven. The game plan seeks to hasten the fall of our Capitalistic-based economy by overloading the bureaucracy with a flood of impossible demands, thus pushing society into crises and economic collapse, paving the way for a new national system.

THE DEGROWTH MOVEMENT

The degrowth movement is an example of the progressive agenda. The degrowth movement supports antipollution policies, a redistribution of income, and is very anti-Capitalistic. In addition, the degrowth movement fosters the idea that the economy cannot grow forever because of its finite resources.

Degrowthers believe that growth endangers the ecosystem and undermines the earth's foundations. The idea that growth has limits is not new. Robert Malthus was an economist who wrote a book titled The Principles of Population published in 1798. Malthus postulated that because the population increases geometrically (2, 4, 8, 16, etc.) and the world's food supply can only increase arithmetically (one, two, three, four, etc.), eventually the world will experience mass starvation. However, history has debunked his theory because the population has grown less than geometrically, and the food supply has increased more than arithmetically.

CHAPTER 3: KEY PLAYERS

Degrowthers believe that consumers have used an ever-increasing share of the world's resources because of the increase in population. Therefore, growth endangers the ecosystem and undermines the earth's foundations. Degrowthers are concerned that the most advanced countries are leaving less room for other nations to prosper. Degrowthers do not favor recessions even though they support a shrinking economic pie. They believe that we can manage and control the shrinkage and minimize the ill effects of anti-growth policies. The degrowth movement advances a planned system whereby wealthier nations will experience an economic contraction, eventually reaching a steady-state operating within the earth's limited resources. Degrowthers believe that minor changes to the present system will not suffice. They want to replace the system with a new and different economic system that will liberate the world from the burden of pursuing material excess—stuff that we do not need to live a gratifying life. According to degrowthers, consumerism is a debilitating addiction that degrades nature and prevents humankind from realizing its potential for well-being and true happiness. Degrowth policies support an uncomplicated way of life, whereby we produce and consume fewer goods and services.

United Nations Agendas 21 (1992) and 2030 (2015) shows us how to implement these Sustainable Living goals of the degrowth movement. Agenda 21 offers a detailed plan for Sustainable Development that countries should implement. In 2015, world leaders met in New York City to present a new fifteen-year plan entitled *Transforming Our World: the 2030 Agenda for Sustainable Development*. Agenda 2030 builds upon Agenda 21. The American 2050 Project combines the two by proposing to have every American living in eleven megaregions

CHAPTER 3: KEY PLAYERS

separated by wilderness connected by high-speed trains such as portrayed in the movie *Hunger Games*.

Glenn Beck and Harriet Parke have authored a book titled *Agenda 21 – Into the Shadows*. In the book, they tell the story of a small group of Americans who have escaped the UN compounds where they were required to be obedient residents of autocratic, merciless authorities. In the book, the United Nations has divided the United States into sections where the government has returned the land to nature, and the people live in fenced compounds in a small part of what once was the United States.

The difference between Agenda 21 and Agenda 2030 is that U.N. Agenda 2030 encompasses more than the environment; it calls for governments seizing control of the means of production. U.N. Agenda 2030 specifies how the planners will strictly regulate everything people do to save the planet. The U.N. web page states that all countries and all stakeholders, acting in collaborative partnership, will implement this plan. The persons who favor degrowth policies are planners; they adhere to the belief of world collectivism.

The master plan consists of 17 Post-2015 Sustainable Development Goals (SDGs) with 169 specific targets. "*As we embark on this collective journey, we pledge that no one will be left behind,*" reads the UN manifesto, entitled Transforming Our World. "*This Agenda is a plan of action for people, planet and prosperity,*" reads the preamble. "*All countries and all stakeholders, acting in collaborative partnership, will implement this plan.*"

Our Global Neighborhood - the Report of the Commission on Global Governance is the blueprint for the United Nations plans for a one-world government. The

CHAPTER 3: KEY PLAYERS

publication calls for a world standing army under the command of the UN secretary general, an economic security council combining the World Bank, the International Monetary Fund, the United Nations Development Program, and the World Trade Organization. The publication calls for consolidating these organizations into a unified world-wide banking scheme with a one-world currency.

GEORGIA GUIDESTONES

On a hilltop in Elbert County, Georgia stands a large granite monument. Engraved in eight different languages on the four giant stones are Ten Guides or commandments of the Progressive Movement:

1. Maintain humanity under 500,000,000 in perpetual balance with nature.

2. Guide reproduction wisely – improving fitness and diversity.

3. Unite humanity with a living new language.

4. Rule passion – faith – tradition – and all things with tempered reason.

5. Protect people and nations with fair laws and just courts.

6. Let all nations rule internally resolving external disputes in a world court.

7. Avoid petty laws and useless officials.

8. Balance personal rights with social duties.

9. Prize truth – beauty – love – seeking harmony with the infinite.

10. Be not a cancer on the earth – Leave room for nature – Leave room for nature.

CHAPTER 4:
AUSTRIANS vs KEYNESIANS

The United States is a republic, a political system based on law, tempered by democracy. The purpose of a republic is to protect the minority from the majority. In a pure democracy, the majority of voters could take everything away from the minority; the minority would have no protection. A threat to our freedom comes when society chooses to tip the scales too far in either direction. Too much republic leads to a totalitarian state, and too much democracy favors the majority.

Only white male property owners (about 10 to 16 percent of the population) could vote at the beginning of America's republic. Because all voters had skin in the game, there was less chance that most voters would raid the Treasury. States gradually dropped the property requirements, and eventually, other groups gained the right to vote.

James Madison, known as the father of the Constitution, warned us against making poor choices.

> *"Democracies have ever been spectacles of turbulence and contention; democracies have ever been found incompatible with personal security and*

CHAPTER 4: AUSTRIANS vs KEYNESIANS

> *rights of property, and have in general been as short in their lives as they have been violent in their deaths."*

Alexander Hamilton was a Founding Father, soldier, economist, political philosopher, one of America's first constitutional lawyers and the first Secretary of the Treasury. John Adams was a Founding Father, the second President of the Unites States and the first Vice President.

> Alexander Hamilton: *"We are a republican form of government. We will never achieve real liberty in despotism or the extremes of democracy."*
>
> John Adams: *"Democracy never lasts long. It soon wastes, exhausts and murders itself. There never was a democracy yet that did not commit suicide."*

John Stuart Mill, an economist who lived in the 1800s, recognized that the market system was about the production of goods and services, it was not about the distribution of goods and services. In his famous book, *Principles of Political Economy*, published in 1848, Mill states:

> *"The things once there, humankind individually or collectively, can do with them as they please. They can place them at the disposal of whomever they please, and on whatever terms. . . . Even what a person has produced by his individual toil, unaided by anyone, he*

CHAPTER 4: AUSTRIANS vs KEYNESIANS

> *cannot keep, unless by the permission of society. . . . The distribution of wealth, therefore, depends on the laws and customs of society."*

Yes, we can choose to redistribute goods and services, but will this redistribution lead to inefficiencies? When does redistribution impede growth and impair productivity? If the government interferes with the price mechanism too much, price signals blur, confusion sets in, and the economy shrinks. Because things wear out, we have to grow to take advantage of new technology and replace what we have lost. We need capital to grow, but who should do the investing? Crony capitalism exists when business success depends on a close relationship between big business and government officials. Rent-seeking is the practice of corporations influencing legislation by way of lobbyists. Rent-seeking is the grease smoothing the relationship between big business and politicians. When corporations lobby Congress to gain political favor and that favor convinces them they will be protected from losses, we have moral hazard. Moral hazard leads to risky investments while it privatizes profits and socializes losses.

GROWTH

If we do not grow, we end up with less and less with each passing day as things deteriorate. That well-running car you drive will eventually need repairs. If we grow by 2 percent, but things deteriorate at a 3 percent rate, we end up with less. Insufficient growth can lead to an unequal distribution of wealth, and civil unrest as the poor receive less of a shrinking pie. The world is experiencing lower birth rates but longer life expectancies than in

CHAPTER 4: AUSTRIANS vs KEYNESIANS

earlier years. The longer life expectancy is why the population has increased from 3 billion 50 years ago to about 7 billion people today! More children are surviving and living to adulthood and old age. Thus we have to grow to stand still on a per capita basis.

Germany offers a compelling example of pro-growth policies under Ludwig Erhard in the 1940s and Gerhard Schröder in recent times. Ludwig Erhard encouraged the elimination of price controls in Germany after World War Two. The abolishment of price controls allowed consumers to express their wants to sellers, and the higher prices encouraged producers to increase production. Along with currency reform and decontrolled prices, the government cut taxes, paving the way to a booming economy. Output continued to grow after 1948, and by 1958, industrial production was more than four times its previous annual rate. Gerhard Schröder, a German chancellor from 1998 to 2005, lowered and simplified the tax code, eliminated many regulations, revamped unemployment benefits, and streamlined labor laws. When funding comes from the government, political goals will supersede growth policies. These pro-growth policies were not to last. Germany chose to adopt high-tax rates, generous public spending programs, and policies restricting competition among corporations. Consequently, incentives to hire new workers, invest in new plants and equipment and take risks diminished.

Since the 1980s, there has been a drop in the number of hours worked, investments, and new technologies. Restrictions that protect incumbent producers have compounded the problem of insufficient growth. For example, France has made free shipping from Amazon illegal to aid French businesses. At the same time, there has been a movement away from private to

CHAPTER 4: AUSTRIANS vs KEYNESIANS

public enterprises. When funding comes from the government, political goals often supersede growth policies.

Growth is the only way out of a country's debt predicament. However, the Keynesian consensus, which has dominated world economic councils, believes growth is primarily a function of government spending (even if it necessitates a tax hike) and that spending cuts are equivalent to lower growth. Moreover, this Keynesian emphasis on public expenditure is a top-down approach to the economy, whereas Austrian economists tend to favor policies that grow the economy from the bottom-up. As a result, Austrians expect ebbs and flow in economic activity and believe that slumps are inevitable.

Austrians support small government, and Keynesians favor big government. Austrians see a problem when governments are intrusive and unpredictable. Despite these shortcomings, Keynesian policies are the norm today. President Ronald Reagan supported Austrian economics in the 1980s and was a student of F.A. Hayek. He often warned us against planned economies and often quoted F.A. Hayek's book *The Road to Serfdom*. In the 1980s, some governments made reforms that encouraged private investment, an end to price controls, and lower tax rates. Since the economic crisis of 2007-2008, the activist ideas of Keynesians have overshadowed the free market ideas of Austrians while debt levels have climbed dramatically. Consider this, one million seconds is four days, one billion seconds is 32 years, and one trillion seconds is 32,000 years! A large national debt stifles growth as more resources go to service the debt, especially when the money goes to foreigners and the super wealthy. The high debt also makes countries vulnerable to rising interest rates, especially for low income persons.

CHAPTER 4: AUSTRIANS vs KEYNESIANS

In the *Road to Serfdom*, Friedrich Hayek compares the modern man to a serf in the middle ages. Life was tenuous during the middle ages, and the typical person was eager for security. The feudal system attached the serf to the land and required him to work for a part of the year and to bear arms in exchange for protection. Thus, the serf relinquished his freedom for security.

We have to choose to have more freedom or more security. Where could you live without worry or concern? Yes, you guessed it, in prison! However, security comes at a price, and that price is a loss of personal freedom. You cannot succeed in life unless you are free to fail; risk-taking, failure, disappointment, and loss are the ingredients for success. If you are not free to fail, then you are not free to succeed. Hayek warned that centralized planning that limits competition leads to tyranny, serfdom, and economic stagnation. As long as voters look to the government to protect them, governments can oblige by eliminating competition, entrepreneurship, innovation, and consumer sovereignty, resulting in insufficient growth and serfdom. Friedrich Hayek warned us against economic policies in the name of social justice. Thousands of organizations have in their mission statement that they aim to improve social justice. Hayek believed that social justice is a term that means anything a group wants it to mean, and it is an excuse to limit freedom and redistribute wealth.

Global prosperity requires fundamental change, and that change is impossible without suffering. Yet, instead of planners going with the flow and changing their policies as conditions change, they tend to fix their specified goals on specified dates, regardless of changing events. On January 28, 1986, even though engineers predicted failure, NASA managers authorized the launch of the Challenger spacecraft to meet the deadline; the

CHAPTER 4: AUSTRIANS vs KEYNESIANS

shuttle exploded 73 seconds into its flight. According to Hayek, events like these are inevitable. Keynesians argue that our problems are more primarily political. If the crisis were economic, we could reduce corporate tax rates and red tape to encourage investment and risk-taking. Instead, in their eagerness to embrace the ideas of Keynesian economics, policymakers neglected Austrian policies. Austrians believe politicians will not fix the economy because they are beholden to special interests and the deep state.

Lawlessness occurs when there is a disconnect between legal entities. Some agencies have limits to their authority, while others have almost none. For example, when the Labor Department wants to make rule changes, it must go through a cost-benefit analysis and submit its proposals to the executive branch for review. But for the Internal Revenue Service (IRS), this is not the case. A 1983 memorandum between the Treasury Department and the Office of Management and Budget exempts the IRS from submitting any rules change to the executive branch. Despite attempts by Congress to gain oversight over the IRS, IRS bureaucrats still impose some of their policies. This independence of the IRS impedes the economic agenda of eliminating onerous fines and complicated forms.

California's attorney general has supported California law that imposes a $10,000 fine on any employer cooperating with federal agents by giving them employee information. He acknowledged that the federal government has jurisdiction to enforce immigration laws but said the new state law seeks to protect workers' privacy. California has declared itself a sanctuary state in opposition to federal law. In addition, San Francisco has passed an ordinance prohibiting city employees from using city funds or resources to assist federal immigration

CHAPTER 4: AUSTRIANS vs KEYNESIANS

authorities. Problems can also arise when there is a disconnect between market forces and authoritarian rule. Because Austrians believe that growth stems from savings and investing, they oppose the Federal Reserve's policy of keeping interest rates artificially low. Mandated low-interest rates discourage savings. Keynesians, on the other hand, believe that low interest rates will encourage demand. Keynesians believe that as long as we can manage demand—we can manage the economy.

Economists favor low and steady growth because once the rate of growth slows the economy can slip into a recession. Brendan Miniter is the author of *The 4% Solution*. In the book, he claims that a 4% growth rate can solve our economic problems. We can raise wages, clean the environment, achieve full employment, pursue clean energy sources, and protect individual liberties, but only if we sufficiently grow. If we grow 5 percent, we can put 2 percent more resources toward social programs and still have a healthy 3% surplus. In *The Endgame: The End of The Debt Supercycle and How It Changes Everything*, John Mauldin suggests that nature can teach us something. Some California counties have full-time firefighters to fight small forest fires. Other counties have no full-time firefighters and let small fires burn. Counties with full-time firefighters have fewer fires, but they tend to be large when they do have fires. Mauldin concludes that when the government tries to fend off every downturn, slumps are less frequent, but it tends to be severe once in a recession.

FULL EMPLOYMENT

The Bureau of Labor Statistics defines unemployment as persons actively seeking employment. Therefore, we cannot have

CHAPTER 4: AUSTRIANS vs KEYNESIANS

zero percent unemployment because someone is always looking for work. The Bureau of Labor Statistics considers the economy fully employed when 4 to 6 percent of the labor force is seeking employment. The Full Employment Act of 1946 mandates the federal government to predict the employment rate for the next fiscal year. Congress must submit full employment policies if the projected rate is less than full employment. Austrian economists have objections to this act for the following reasons:

- Business cycles are natural and therefore we should allow them to run their course without allowing federal mandates to cause disruptions.
- Government policies tend to be pro-cyclical rather than countercyclical, meaning they can accentuate the wide swings of the business cycle instead of smoothing them out.
- Forecasting future activity can be difficult, if not impossible.

A change came in 1978 with the Full Employment and Balanced Growth Act, also known as the Humphrey-Hawkins Full Employment Act. With this act, Congress put mandates on the Fed to ensure both price stability and full employment. Austrians object to this dual mandate because the cure for inflation is to reduce the money supply, and the solution for unemployment is to increase the money supply. However, the Fed cannot fight both problems simultaneously when we experience stagflation, as we did in the 1970s. Austrians call this a feel-good policy because it sounds good, but it can defy

CHAPTER 4: AUSTRIANS vs KEYNESIANS

economic rules. At times, the Fed has admitted that its policies are counterproductive, but the law forced it to do something. The Fed effectively fights inflation because when it decreases the money supply, people have no choice but to spend less. However, the Fed cannot force people to borrow money, limiting its usefulness when unemployment is the problem. Austrians support ending this dual mandate and favor liberating the central bank to focus on stabilizing prices.

Economists define inflation as an increase in the average price level. A small amount of inflation is not harmful, significantly if people accurately predict it, and it occurs regularly. However, inflation can cause problems if it exceeds 5 percent a year and is unpredictable. High and unanticipated inflation can lead to unemployment because it can diminish consumers' buying power and thwarts risk-taking. Nevertheless, people still come to America because they believe that our economic system is fair and rewards hard work. However, the concept of fairness can be a relative thing. Is it fair that some people have more money than others? Should society choose to strive to have an even distribution of income?

A weakness of the free market system is that it cannot guarantee safe working conditions and a clean environment. Unsafe working conditions and pollution are examples of negative externalities, which are unpleasant by-products of the industrial process. The only solution to pollution is for the federal government to impose environmental regulations on all corporations, putting every company on a level playing field. The challenge is to promote a clean environment without sabotaging growth. All economists favor a clean environment, but they disagree on the specifics.

CHAPTER 4: AUSTRIANS vs KEYNESIANS

Although we cannot minimize pollution without government intervention, government overreach can be a problem when a single person is in charge of an agency. For example, the debate has long existed over the effectiveness and fairness of the U.S. Environmental Protection Agency. Traditionally, the EPA has first considered regulations from a scientific perspective, economics comes in second, legal considerations third, and politics a distant fourth. Politics is the most crucial consideration, legalities second, technology third, and economics a distant fourth. The government cannot create jobs, guarantee growth, or establish security. It can only redistribute what the economy produces. If the economy grows less, society receives less. The more government forces regulations and taxes on productive people, the more obstacles to a healthy economy.

FREEDOM AND THE NATIONAL DEBT

The federal government borrows money by selling bonds and securities, which is an agreement between the borrower and the lender regarding the amount, the interest rate, and the maturity date. The deficit is an annual figure, and the debt is total indebtedness. Excessive debt leads to fewer choices as more of people's income goes to servicing the debt. Imagine servicing a 30 trillion dollar national debt when interest rates increase! The Fed can only influence interest rates. It cannot control interest rates over the long run. The Fed controls only the federal funds rate and the prime rate; market forces determine all other interest rates. Keynesians will raise taxes on the wealthy to pay for social programs because they believe that the tax increase will not stifle

CHAPTER 4: AUSTRIANS vs KEYNESIANS

growth. Austrians believe that increasing taxes beyond a certain point will discourage investments and lead to slower growth.

CHAPTER 5:
GOVERNMENT OVERREACH

The federal government took over public education with the No Child Left Behind Law and the Common Core Curriculum. The No Child Left Behind Act authorized several federal education programs administered by the states. Under the 2002 law, states were required to test reading and math in grades three through eight and once in high school. The Every Student Succeeds Act (ESSA) replaced the No Child Left Behind Act in 2015. The ESSA retains the annual standardized testing requirements of the No Child Left Behind Act but shifts the law's federal accountability provisions to states. The states are also left to determine the consequences of low-performing schools. Common Core has influenced a whole generation to value fairness over opportunity—rote memory over cognitive thinking. To revert to local control of education will be difficult because states have committed themselves to the status quo.

The U.S. Department of Education put out a memo in July of 2009. The notice stated that states leading the way on school reform would be eligible to compete for $4.35 billion in Race to the Top competitive grants to support education reform and innovation in classrooms. The stipulation was that once a

CHAPTER 5: GOVERNMENT OVERREACH

state accepted the money, it had to abide by the common core standards. Not all states joined the 45 states and the District of Columbia in adopting the standards. Governor Rick Perry stated, *"Texas is on the right path toward improved education, and we would be foolish and irresponsible to place our children's future in the hands of unelected bureaucrats and special interest groups thousands of miles away in Washington, virtually eliminating parents' participation in their children's education."*

An early backing of the Common Core proposal came from the Bill and Melinda Gates Foundation that plans on spending billions of dollars in public education and is committed to helping build political support across the country, persuading state governments to join the program. The Gates Foundation spread money across the political spectrum to entities including the teacher's unions, the American Federation of Teachers and the National Education Association, and business organizations such as the U.S. Chamber of Commerce. Money flowed to groups that promoted uniform standards. The Gates Foundation also agreed to pay for the new textbooks.

Bill Gates and others like him are technocrats; they are not so much interested in education as they are interested in the power of technology. They see technology to influence people's opinions about such things as fairness and the environment they want to shape the world by their beliefs. The purpose of present-day education is to replace cognitive thinking with sociology and ideology under social justice. When the Gates Foundation hired lobbyists in Washington, the lobbyists convinced politicians to overreach into the area of public education. Events have moved us from a knowledge-based mastery achievement system to a system that demands uniformity—the system teaches students to fear descent from the mainstream narrative and be intolerant of

CHAPTER 5: GOVERNMENT OVERREACH

opposing viewpoints. Moreover, because Christianity is opposed to the expansion of state power over people's lives and supports the concept of the individual, which is the smallest minority, rather than the collective, it is a prime target of the modern-day progressive movement. The idea that the government would mandate schools to teach things like transsexuality and homosexual marriage would have been inconceivable years ago. Now not only is it accepted but it is encouraged. The Every Student Succeeds Act weaves sex education into every subject; even math uses story problems dealing with sexual topics! The classics are mostly gone in the humanities to be replaced by social issues with a liberal bias.

Rachel Carson Middle School in Herndon, Virginia, is full of winners. The school won a governor's award for teaching excellence for 2007 to 2011, and the national forum for middle-school improvement cited Rachel Carson as a school to watch. However, the federal government considers Rachel Carson a failure because it does not fit its definition of success as improvement in test scores of different groups. Rachel Carson has high average scores but fails because it has achievement gaps when it breaks out test results by such categories as race, gender, and income.

Corinthian College was a college with more than 100 campuses. Private colleges, like Corinthian, specialize in training students for blue-collar jobs, jobs like driving big commercial trucks, nursing, cloud computing, web development, database programming, software development, and network security, offering degrees in healthcare, business, criminal justice, transportation technology, construction trades, and information technology. Corinthian College was a for-profit college and one of the largest for-profit post-secondary education companies in

CHAPTER 5: GOVERNMENT OVERREACH

North America. Because the college failed to meet government mandates promptly, the Department of Education put it out of business. First, the government restricted federal funding access because of inadequate marketing, excessive dropout and student loan default rates, and unfulfilled promises. Because 80% of Corinthians' revenue came from federal funding, $1.4 billion in federal financial aid each year, this action was a death blow to the college. Second, the Consumer Financial Protection Bureau (CFPB) wiped out company shareholders and creditors by accusing the college of predatory lending. The government claimed that Corinthian used aggressive collection efforts by suspending students who failed to meet their loan obligations. The government's third complaint concerns paying staff bonuses for collecting past-due payments from students. A fourth complaint was that not enough graduates found full-time employment in their chosen field.

Another casualty for the same reasons was the ITT Technical Institute. ITT was a technical institute that operated for a profit with 130 campuses in 38 states and was operational for 50 years. On September 26, 2016, ITT Tech abruptly shut down, leaving 35,000 students without a degree and 8,000 employees without a job. The reasons for the closure are the same as with Corinthian College, financial sanctions by the U.S. Department of Education. The Department of Education claimed that ITT was charging tens of thousands of dollars in tuition but failing to provide valuable education to its students.

A third casualty occurred in June of 2016 when the Department of Education forced the Accrediting Council for Independent Colleges and Schools (ACICS) shutdown. The Department of Education officially stripped the ACICS of its authority, handing down the final blow in a long controversy over

CHAPTER 5: GOVERNMENT OVERREACH

the council's ability to be an effective watchdog for students and billions of taxpayer dollars. ACICS accredited 245 colleges that enrolled 800,000 students.

The Department of Education is now judging all colleges and universities on graduation and retention rates, the ability of graduates to pay back their student loans, the school's accessibility to low-income students, and their ability to hold down costs. The government will tie federal funds to the ratings. Consequently, authorities are imposing funding models that take into account performance measures related to student outcomes. Funding models specify the number of students earning one or more awards in a given academic year, the number of students from underserved populations who receive recognition, and the number of students who complete a degree within six years of starting college.

The Tenth Amendment of the U.S. Constitution reads: *"The powers not delegated to the United States by the Constitution, nor prohibited by it to the States, are reserved to the States respectively, or to the people."* The Tenth Amendment leaves the power to create schools and a system for education in the hands of individual states, rather than the federal government. Consequently, states and local school boards had to be convinced to relinquish their independence and allow government overreach.

GOVERNMENT PROGRAMS

Government programs such as Social Security, Medicare, Medicaid, and food stamps have contributed to America's rising national debt since the early 1970s. Congress often raises the

CHAPTER 5: GOVERNMENT OVERREACH

debt ceiling to accommodate the increase in government spending. These programs are contributors to spending and debt because they always start with narrow eligibility requirements, but Congress relaxes them over time. With each expansion, Congress uses it as the base for the subsequent increase. An example of government overreach is Medicaid, a social safety net program pushing many states to financial ruin. What started as a narrowly tailored program to cover the health care needs of low-income people has grown into a massive entitlement program that now includes many healthy Americans. The increase in Medicaid spending also hurts the people most in need of assistance because as the Medicaid population increases, there may be less money for each person.

Before we can slow the process of government overreach, we must recognize the problem, both political parties have to agree on the remedy, and the President has to be a strong leader and must communicate his economic agenda to all Americans. A book on the subject is *The High Cost of Good Intentions,* 2017, by John F. Cogan.

THE DODD-FRANK ACT

The Dodd-Frank Act of 2010, also known as the Financial Reform Bill or the Wall Street Reform and Consumer Protection Act, is about 2,300 pages. Congress designed the act to make banks safer by limiting banks' ability to take risks and forces them to increase their liquidity. The Federal Reserve is to administer stress tests each year for any bank with more than $50 billion worth of assets. The Dodd-Frank Act is more about protecting the banking industry from a crash and less about preventing the subsequent crises. The Dodd-Frank law impacts

CHAPTER 5: GOVERNMENT OVERREACH

growth by increasing regulations on selected businesses. For example, J.P. Morgan hired 10,000 compliance officers to handle its mandates. According to the Federal Deposit Insurance Corporation, more than a thousand commercial banks have disappeared because of the Dodd-Frank Law. Government figures also indicate that the country is losing community banks and credit unions because of government regulations. Dodd-Frank was supposed to limit mortgage risk by establishing standards, but these requirements have been ineffectual partly because mortgage transactions by Fannie Mae and Freddie Mac are exempt. Fannie and Freddie are government-sponsored enterprises that play a significant role in the mortgage industry. Both Fannie and Freddie buy mortgages from lenders, pool them together, and sell them as mortgage-backed securities to investors.

The banks, which the government considers too big to fail, and therefore too big to jail, are protected by the Dodd-Frank Law. These banks make up about 60% of GDP, and they control nearly 50% of all bank deposits. The four nonbank financial firms designated initially as systematically necessary are MetLife, American International Group (AIG), Prudential Insurance, and General Electric. These corporations must have enough money on hand as a capital cushion. The challenge for these companies is staying within the limits of the law while enhancing shareholder value. General Electric divested itself of its financial unit, and MetLife moved to shed a chunk of its U.S. life insurance business. In 2017, the Financial Stability Oversight Council voted to free AIG from being a systemically important financial institution. This vote freed the insurance company from stricter oversight by the federal government, such as tighter

CHAPTER 5: GOVERNMENT OVERREACH

capital rules, federal approval of mergers, and placement of government examiners at the firm.

BAIL-INS

The Todd-Frank Law has given banks the right to confiscate depositors' money when bankruptcy threatens. In a bailout, the government makes creditors whole by using taxpayers' money. With a bail-in, big banks can recapitalize themselves with the savings of their creditors. In other words, the Todd-Frank Law has given banks the right to confiscate depositors' money in an attempt to make them whole when bankruptcy threatens. However, there is not enough money in depositor's accounts and pension funds to cover the volume of debt. Legally, when you deposit money in a bank, you are an unsecured creditor. According to the Dodd-Frank Law, the derivative holdings of big American banks, which are several times greater than the world's GDP, come first in the event of a collapse. The Bank of International Settlements in Basel, Switzerland, the central bank for central banks, has sanctioned bail-ins. Banks in Argentina and Cyprus have confiscated depositor's money. Cyprus banks were over-leveraged to the point that their liabilities exceeded the country's GDP.

FSOC and CFPB

The Dodd-Frank Law created the Financial Stability Oversight Council (FSOC) and the Consumer Financial Protection Bureau (CFPB). The FSOC can declare a financial firm systemically important based on any risk-related factors that it considers appropriate. Companies tagged with this designation

CHAPTER 5: GOVERNMENT OVERREACH

are subject to an increase in government regulation. The CFPB jurisdiction includes banks, credit unions, securities firms, payday lenders, mortgage-servicing operations, foreclosure relief services, debt collectors, and other financial companies operating in the United States. The CFPB is more concerned with the safety of consumers more than the soundness of banks. It can punish lenders who in good faith offer loans that the bureau later believes to be unfair, deceptive, or abusive. These open-ended standards set no limits on the regulator's power.

Authors of the U.S. Constitution chose to give Congress the power of the purse to check against excessive Executive overreach and prohibited the establishment of independent rogue agencies. However, in 2010, President Obama decided to defy this provision when he decreed by executive order that the Federal Reserve would house and finance the Consumer Financial Protection Bureau. Because Congress does not fund the agency, it does not have authority over it. As a result, the CFPB promotes big government by politicizing decisions and helps undermine aspects of the free market, and is at odds with the separation of power.

The CFPB has chosen to use the concept of disparate impact to assess financial institutions. Disparate impact holds that government bureaucrats can declare a business practice unfair and illegal if it has a disproportionate adverse impact on members of a minority group. In other words, the CFPB can penalize a business even though no one brings a discrimination charge against the corporation. For example, if the employees' makeup does not adhere to the racial or ethnic mix that the CFBP mandates, the CFPB can declare the firm guilty of discrimination. And how does the CFPB determine the ethnic

CHAPTER 5: GOVERNMENT OVERREACH

mix? One way is for them to consider the employee's last names and guess their nationality.

The Consumer Financial Protection Bureau imposes fines and fees on financial institutions, but Congress does not require the CFPB to transfer the money to the Treasury. The agency has collected billions of dollars from businesses, but the agency's head determines what happens to that money. The CFPB prefers to help some groups but not others, thus giving way to ideological preference. When the government makes guesses like this, the effects on freedom and economic growth are profound. If a bank lends money and the loan goes bad, regulators may charge the bank with fraud. On the other hand, if the bank makes a high return, regulators may deem it too profitable at the expense of a minority class of people.

Dodd-Frank does not honor checks and balances; it eliminates them. The problem with Dodd-Frank is that an unelected council has the power to rewrite the rules of insurance over the objections of insurers, insurance regulators, and Congress. A certain amount of flexibility is necessary for a law, but before Dodd-Frank, the powers that Congress granted to regulators were limited. As a result, there was a consistency in policy because regulators had to be responsive to Congress. The Dodd-Frank Law replaces this predictability with uncertainty and fear and imposes demands on institutions never contemplated by Congress. The Constitution empowers the President and Congress, and the courts to prevent regulators from issuing arbitrary or discriminatory regulations. However, Dodd-Frank does not honor checks and balances; it eliminates them. Instead, Dodd-Frank prohibits Congress from reviewing its budget. In addition, when the Consumer Financial Protection Bureau deems a financial institution too big to fail, the Financial Stability

CHAPTER 5: GOVERNMENT OVERREACH

Oversight Council blocks the courts from ruling whether the regulators correctly interpreted the law.

The Financial Stability Oversight Council can declare a nonbank financial firm as a systematically important financial institution that subjects it to heightened supervision by the Federal Reserve Board of Governors, making a mockery of property rights and due process. The FSOC can now threaten large financial institutions with systemic risk designation with no real avenue for defense. Moreover, the identification gives the government a say in some business decisions made by the financial institutions, including new requirements beyond written corporate laws or existing financial regulations.

The Consumer Financial Protection Bureau's and the Financial Stability Oversight Council's constitutional violations are not merely the focus of law-school debates; they pose a direct threat to economic recovery. Community banks are afraid of lending money because the CFPB might later decide that the loans were unfair. American finance is becoming more political, less vibrant, and further removed from law principles. Regulators can take over a struggling bank and every affiliate in the bank's network by claiming that it may default and that its default could adversely affect the nation's stability. The original purpose of the CFPB is sound. Its mission to protect and empower consumers, promote fair and competitive markets, and stabilize the financial system are noble and worthwhile goals. But poorly designed regulations choke off access to credit, cause higher interest rates and limit consumer choice.

The federal government and much of the financial system could not function without the help of private accounting corporations such as Promontory, Deloitte,

CHAPTER 5: GOVERNMENT OVERREACH

PricewaterhouseCoopers, and Ernst & Young. Regulators and banks hire these firms to investigate suspicious activity, act as intermediaries between the government and private companies and advise financial institutions on complying with complex regulatory rules. Promontory is arguably the most influential of these regulators and can receive up to $1,500 an hour for its services.

The whistleblower provision and legal protection are two features of the Dodd-Frank Law. Employees who believe that their company violates the law can contact the authorities with specifics. At this point, the law protects an employee from retaliation. If, after an investigation, the federal authorities find any illegalities, like fraud or tax evasion, the whistleblower gets to keep from 10 to 30 percent of any monies collected. The law also requires courts to grant the bureau deference regarding its interpretation of the federal consumer financial law. The House Financial Services Committee has voted 34 to 26 along party lines to undo significant parts of the Dodd-Frank Law and called for restructuring the Consumer Financial Protection Bureau. The legislation relieves banks of some regulatory requirements as long as they meet their capital standards. The rollback also requires banks to go through stress tests every two years instead of every year.

No one has started a new bank since Congress enacted the Dodd-Frank Law. The lack of law principles, the arbitrary and opaque decision-making process by a few officials with near-absolute authority, and the emphasis on politics over economics have stifled growth. Small start-up businesses, the lifeblood of the American economy, have been adversely affected by the demise of local banks. The dynamic effect of these laws generates a moral hazard. It distorts the behavior of market

CHAPTER 5: GOVERNMENT OVERREACH

participants in a way that contradicts the principles of free and open markets while favoring only the largest financial institutions. Meanwhile, these laws allow the American consumer with fewer choices, higher costs, more paperwork when applying for a loan, and liability for a financial collapse. According to the Federal Reserve Bank of Richmond, the federal government backs 60 percent of the weaknesses in America's financial markets in one way or another. These changes lead to a concentration of power; they are trading economic growth for perceived security and making the U.S. economy less vibrant.

According to the National Association of Manufacturers, federal regulations cost the U.S. more than 12% of the gross domestic product and $20,000 per employee per year to satisfy regulations. This burden on manufacturers effectively raises the cost of hiring full-time employees and has led to more part-time jobs. These excessive regulations also put American producers at a competitive disadvantage with some foreign competitors and have forced American companies to relocate to foreign countries by either buying a competitor and moving their domicile overseas or selling themselves to a competitor.

PROPERTY RIGHTS

Thomas Jefferson argued that our rights are a gift from God. Judge Andrew Napolitano has a video titled *A Nation of Sheep*, which is the title of one of his books. In the video, he explains the Stamp Act before the Revolutionary War. Every piece of paper in a person's home had to have a picture, a stamp, of the king. How did the king's government know if people were abiding by this law? The English Parliament passed the Writs of Assistance Act. This act allowed British soldiers to write search

CHAPTER 5: GOVERNMENT OVERREACH

warrants. Therefore, a British soldier could appear at your door and authorize himself to examine the contents of your home. If the soldiers found anything without the official stamp, soldiers would confiscate the property. The Stamp Act was a catalyst that led to the Declaration of Independence.

When Thomas Jefferson wrote the Declaration of Independence, with the help of James Madison, he affirmed the natural rights of man. The Declaration says that: *"We are endowed by our creator with certain rights, that among them are life, liberty, and the pursuit of happiness."* The purpose of the Constitution is to keep the government in check, to divide and diffuse power among the different branches of government.

Alexander Hamilton and John Adams believed that our rights come from the government and not from God and that we only have the rights that the government gives us. However, it was Jefferson and Madison who prevailed. The first amendment does not say the government shall grant us the freedom of speech; it stipulates that Congress shall make no law abridging the freedom of speech. Thus, the first amendment presumes that the freedom of speech preexisted Congress, and it came from somewhere else; it came from God and not from the government.

The fourth amendment is critical; it restricts the government's authority over us regarding the right to privacy. The government cannot invade your home without written probable cause by an impartial judge. The fourth amendment puts a neutral judge between the government and the person. During the presidency of John Adams, when Thomas Jefferson was Vice President and the country was only eight years old, Congress passed the Alien and Sedition Act, which, among other things, made it a crime to criticize the president and members of

CHAPTER 5: GOVERNMENT OVERREACH

Congress. When Thomas Jefferson became president and the Alien and Sedition Act came up for renewal, he refused to renew it.

Congress wrote the Foreign Intelligence Surveillance Act (FISA) in 1977. FISA said that if the target is an agent of a foreign government, then the government does not need the probable cause specified by the Fourth Amendment. Under FISA, the Fourth Amendment still protects citizens. Congress passed the Right to Financial Privacy Act in 1978, bringing us almost full circle from the Writs of Assistance Act. This Act permits government agents to write search warrants and to serve them on financial institutions.

All of this set the stage for the government to pound the final nail into the coffin of liberty. The tragedy of September 2011 and the twin towers' destruction prompted Congress to pass the Patriot Act. The Patriot Act allows the FBI to invade your home when you are not there. The FBI can search the house and even plant listening devices without your knowledge. If the FBI writes a search warrant on your bank account, it is a crime for the bank to tell you of this invasion. This Act shreds the protection given to us by the first and fourth amendments to the Constitution. Meanwhile, it is unlawful for the bank to inform you of any one of these activities. The banker cannot tell his lawyer, spouse, or even a judge in a federal court about the self-written search warrant against you. The penalty for talking is a five-year prison sentence. The Patriot Act limited the search warrants to financial institutions.

On September 13, 2003, three years after the twin towers incident, President George W. Bush signed the Intelligence Authorization Act for Fiscal 2004. Hidden deep in the act is a

CHAPTER 5: GOVERNMENT OVERREACH

definition of financial institutions. A financial institution can be a bank, a trusted company, a credit union, a delicatessen, a restaurant, a hotel, a casino, a travel agency, your lawyer's office, your doctor's office, your telephone company, your internet provider, and the post office, virtually everything but your home.

FALSE FLAGS

There is controversy over what happened on September 11, 2011, when planes hit the twin towers, and 2,977 people died. The official story is that an extremist group hijacked airplanes and carried out suicide attacks. What is difficult to believe is that the planes were also responsible for the destruction of Building Seven, a 47-story skyscraper (each floor the size of a football field) that was a part of the World Trade Center. It took ten seconds for the building to collapse in its footprint, yet no plane hit the building. If the story is true, it would be the first case where a steel-framed building collapsed because of fire. It is also interesting that the 9/11 Commission Report did not mention Building seven, and it took seven years for the federal government to issue a report for Building 7.

A False Flag is a covert operation of an organization designed to deceive the public in such a way as to place the blame on an innocent third party. It concocts a problem, stirs a reaction, then proposes a solution. The term comes from the old days of wooden ships when one ship would hang the flag of its enemy before attacking another ship in its navy to blame the enemy. There are many examples of false flag attacks throughout history. For example, the Reichstag fire was the watershed event that justified Hitler's seizure of power and the suspension of personal liberties.

CHAPTER 5: GOVERNMENT OVERREACH

Whether you accept the official story of 9/11 or you believe it was a false flag incident, there is no dispute about what happened afterward. The occurrence led to the Patriot Act, which empowered the federal government while trashing personal liberties. The enormity of the incident and the fear of a foreign aggressor made Americans give up some of their freedom for more security.

Ole Dammegard has devoted his life to exposing and predicting false flag occurrences. He was awarded the Prague Peace Prize in 2016 and has been a featured speaker at numerous conferences worldwide. Among many other predictions, he warned the world about the attack on the London Bridge in 2017, one month before it happened. He has named the types of targets and the dates of the attacks.

PART-TIME WORK and OBAMACARE

The way Americans finance health care changed when Congress passed the Affordable Care Act in 2010. Many businesses, to avoid penalties, fired full-time employees and hired part-time workers who work less than 30 hours a week. The Internal Revenue Code defines part-time employees as those who work 1,000 hours or less in 12 months; this equivocates to 30 hours a week. These events have led to a decrease in covered employees, full-time employees with full benefits, and increased non-covered employees, part-time employees without benefits. As more Americans work part-time, living standards diminish.

CHAPTER 5: GOVERNMENT OVERREACH

UNREASONABLE POLLUTION LAWS

If a business owner has a social conscience and invests in anti-pollution devices, costs increase, forcing an increase in prices, giving competitors an advantage. Consequently, a company will choose to pollute to keep costs down. The government can solve the problem only when it regulates all polluters. However, what happens when the regulations are too harsh? What happens when policymakers have little knowledge of economics and ignore growth? Government policies can hinder productivity by raising costs, entangling businesses in excessive regulations, and encourage rent-seeking by large firms. Coal-fired plants currently provide power for one-half of the population. Yet, the Environmental Protection Agency (EPA) has forced many coal-fired power plants to shut down because it supports alternative energy sources like solar power, natural gas, and wind power.

Ian Rutherford Pilmer, an Australian geologist, professor emeritus of earth sciences at the University of Melbourne, has published many scientific papers, authored six books, writes and talks on the hoax of global warming. He emphasizes that the earth's temperature has always been in flux and that carbon dioxide is a natural gas that is the basis of all life on earth. He explains how the belief in climate change has become a part of a new kind of morality. A movie on the subject is *Great Global Warming Swindle*, 2007.

THE RULE-OF-LAW COMPROMISED

When the federal government bailed out General Motors in 2009, it ignored current bankruptcy laws and picked the

CHAPTER 5: GOVERNMENT OVERREACH

winners and losers. The government paid auto unions in full because of their generous political contributions but short-changed bondholders and the non-union members at Delphi, GM's former parts subsidiary. Delphi, which underwent one of the largest corporate bankruptcies in U.S. history, lost all of its health and life insurance benefits, and 70,000 retirees lost 65% of their benefits. When government intervenes on an ad-hoc basis, it introduces uncertainty into the mix. Trouble begins when businesses spend less money on research and development and more on rent-seeking. This partnership between big business and government is an example of crony capitalism, which is a destructive force, undermining the economy and political system and the foundations of our culture.

SARBANES-OXLEY ACT

The Sarbanes-Oxley Accounting Reform Act in 2002 rewrote accounting and disclosure rules for publicly traded companies. The purpose of the Act is to prevent business scandals, a noble pursuit. The Act has given the federal government more power to intervene in credit markets. The danger is that the bill has allowed the government to impose penalties on selected companies of its choosing. Sarbanes-Oxley established the Accounting Oversight Board and mandated corporations to deliver internal management reports to the board. Executives who approve unsubstantiated records face fines of up to $5 million and 20 years in prison. Section 404 requires costly external audits of companies, apart from the company's financial statements. Sarbanes-Oxley is the most visible sign of excessive regulation and government overreach and a reason foreign companies forgo U.S. public listing. Large firms can absorb the

CHAPTER 5: GOVERNMENT OVERREACH

high costs of compliance because they have the advantage of economies of scale, whereas smaller businesses cannot meet compliance costs. Congress has exempted companies with less than $75 million of assets to lessen the burden on small businesses.

PATIENT PROTECTION AND AFFORDABLE CARE ACT

Obamacare extends protection to millions of people by expanding Medicaid, accepting people with pre-existing conditions, and subsidizing qualified people to help them buy insurance from companies in the government-run exchange. Policies offered on the exchange have to adhere to one of four government plans. The bill establishes a panel of experts who have the authority to determine the limits of government reimbursements for qualified people. As of this date, the majority of participants receive the subsidy. A Boston University/Harvard Medical School study suggests that Obamacare has shifted up to 80% of people's private insurance onto Medicaid. However, less than 50 percent of doctors are accepting new Medicaid patients because they often lose money. With fewer doctors, patients have to wait longer to see a doctor.

LONG AND COMPLEX BILLS

No person could comprehend the 2,700-page health bill or the 2,300-page financial reform bill before it became law. Nobody understood the 6,000 page Clean Power Plan that commands states to cut carbon emissions by 32% from 2005 levels by 2030. Bills and mandates like these have fostered an atmosphere of uncertainty and fear that erodes investments,

CHAPTER 5: GOVERNMENT OVERREACH

economic growth and diminishes productivity gains. Such laws can change regulators into central planning authorities. Friedrich Hayek warned against the ill effects of planning; tyranny results when rules rule instead of people. Regulators erroneously believe that their models can predict future risk, but they cannot. Besides being ineffective, these complex laws add layers of costs to business expenses.

What is the difference between simple and complex laws? Suppose the government passed a regulation that made it illegal for anyone to wear a tie. Authorities could enforce this law because everyone knows ties. Now let us suppose the government makes it unlawful to wear a beautiful tie. Who is to say what is beautiful? Now the government can define beautiful and can enforce the law however it chooses.

Complex laws expose the American economy to arbitrary decisions. In 1997, Harry Root started Vascular Solutions, a company that invented, manufactured, and sold medical devices. The company grew to 650 employees and one billion dollars in sales. In 2010, a disgruntled employee made a false accusation to the Justice Department about off-label promotion, claiming that a few employees made false claims to potential clients. A grand jury found Harry Root and his company not guilty after the company hired 121 lawyers at the cost of $25 million! Anyone who opposes the DOJ goes against more than 113,000 employees, many lawyers, with an annual budget in the billions. The number of federal regulations is so voluminous that no business can ensure perfect compliance with all the laws. Even a minor transgression can result in multiple lawsuits and billions of dollars in penalties and fines.

CHAPTER 6:
FEDERAL RESERVE

The Federal Reserve is America's central bank. President Woodrow Wilson, and Congress gave up control over the nation's money supply when it transferred authority from the government to the world private banking cabal with the Federal Reserve Act of 1913. A cartel of eight families owns the Federal Reserve and other central banks around the world. They are Goldman Sachs of New York, Rockefeller Brothers of New York, Rothschild Banks of London and Berlin, Lazard Brothers of Paris, Israel Moses Sieff Banks of Italy, Kuhn and Loeb and Company of Germany and New York, and the Warburg Bank of Hamburg and Amsterdam. The Federal Reserve is listed in the telephone book's white pages, while the US Treasury is listed in the yellow pages. Fed employees' email address ends in .org, not .gov.

Commercial banks can multiply money, but only central banks can create money. Before the banking system can multiply money, someone has to make a deposit. But the Federal Reserve does not need a deposit; it can create money by merely pushing a few keys on its computer to credit a client's account by X amount. All currencies are debt instruments; they are floating abstractions that profit the world's bankers. At the top of a dollar bill is printed "Federal Reserve Note." A note is an IOU; it is an agreement to pay interest to the note owner, the Federal Reserve.

CHAPTER 6: FEDERAL RESERVE

Dollars come into existence when the government sells bonds to the Federal Reserve The Bureau of Engraving and Printing of the government converts a small fraction of this borrowed money into physical dollars.

BRETTON WOODS

Seven hundred and thirty delegates attended the Bretton Woods Conference in 1944 from 44 Allied nations to establish an international monetary system. As a result, countries agreed to peg their currencies to gold in a semi-fixed exchange rate system. Thus, the dollar became the standard when America exchanged dollars at $35 per ounce of gold. The Vietnam War and President Lyndon Johnson's Great Society Programs of the 1960s drained the U.S. coffers and increased our national debt—undermining the backing of the dollar by gold. Because the 1970s was a decade of differing inflation rates, it became impossible to trade using fixed exchange rates. President Richard Nixon severed the link to gold when he closed the gold window in August of 1971, disallowing convertibility. This severance from gold was the final blow to the gold standard.

OPEC agreed to sell its oil for dollars in 1975 when America and Saudi Arabia joined forces. America offered military protection and weapons, and Saudi Arabia promised to accept dollars and buy U.S. bonds. Soon other nations followed suit with the Organization of Petroleum Exporting Countries (OPEC) in 1975. The Petrodollar System made the dollar the world's reserve (standard) currency. A turning point came when Saddam Hussein agreed to accept the euro as payment for oil—one year before the attack on the Twin Towers in 2001. Hussein threatened the Petrodollar System, prompting the

CHAPTER 6: FEDERAL RESERVE

Neoconservatives to declare War on Terror and invade Iraq in 2003. By June of 2003, Iraq's oil was once again a part of the Petrodollar System.

America is on the cusp of another paradigm shift, a change at least as fundamental as what happened in 1971. Countries are beginning to sever their tie to the American dollar by finding alternative trade arrangements. So far, 23 nations, representing 60% of the world's GDP, are setting up swaps bypassing the dollar. Russia has announced that they are establishing a clearance system without dollars. This shift away from the dollar may be the most significant event of this era. With China becoming more dependant on foreign oil, China and Saudi Arabia have agreed to a partnership making deals worth billions of dollars, such as building oil refineries in Saudi Arabia. Along with China has massive gold reserves, this cooperation ushers in the new world order as the petro-yuan will replace the American dollar as the world's standard currency and diminish the Saudi-America relationship.

THE FED CREATES MONEY

The U.S. Treasury cannot create new money. Instead, it prints our currency and sells the bills to the Federal Reserve at a discount. The Fed then loans it back to the government at face value plus interest. Therefore, the federal government is dependent upon private bankers to lend it money. Because the Federal Reserve is the federal government's bank, the Fed can also create virtual money by crediting the government's bank account by X number of dollars by simply pushing a few keys on its computer.

CHAPTER 6: FEDERAL RESERVE

The U.S. dollar is a fiat currency because the treasury does not back it with gold or silver. The Constitution contains two sections dealing with monetary issues. Section 8 permits Congress to coin money and regulate its value, and section 10 prohibits states from printing money. The framers intended legal tender to be under the federal government's control, not an independent central bank owned by an international syndicate of bankers—the Federal Reserve is unconstitutional. Bringing back the gold standard would be very hard to do, but boy would it be wonderful. Finally, we'd have a standard on which to base our money.

There have been political reform movements before that have called for a sound money system. In 1900, L. Frank Baum wrote the *Wizard of Oz* as a parable on the Populist Party. This party was independent of the Democrats and Republicans and opposed the concentration of capital by banks and big business. The Yellow Brick Road is the gold standard. The big business supported the gold standard, while reformers favored silver and paper money. Oz is an abbreviation for an ounce of silver, and the Wizard is any president whose power is illusory. Dorothy represents virtuous citizens attracted to radical politics (sound familiar?) because they realized things had gone wrong and that the events needed to change.

COMMERCIAL BANKS AND THE FED

The U.S. banking system consists of a network of privately owned commercial banks and government-sanctioned Federal Reserve Banks. A commercial bank is an institution that accepts demand and savings deposits and makes loans to the public. There are approximately 12,000 commercial banks in

CHAPTER 6: FEDERAL RESERVE

America, but small community banks are going out of business almost every day. Over half of total assets reside in the following six financial institutions: Bank of American Corporation, JP Morgan Chase and Co., Citigroup Inc., Wells Fargo and Co., Goldman Sachs Group Inc., and Morgan Stanley.

BANKING IN AMERICA

At the urging of Alexander Hamilton, Congress established the First Bank of the United States in 1791. Many Americans were uncomfortable with the idea and opposed it. When the bank's 20-year charter expired in 1811, Congress refused to renew it by one vote. In 1816, Congress agreed to charter the Second Bank of the United States by a narrow margin. However, when the country elected Andrew Jackson as president in 1828, he vowed to kill the bank. Citizens supported his attack on the bank, and when the Second Bank's charter expired in 1836, he did not renew it. In 1893, a bank panic triggered a depression; the economy stabilized only after financial mogul J.P. Morgan. Some people wondered what would happen if there was no J.P. Morgan to bail the country out in the subsequent crises. It was clear that the banking and financial system needed serious attention. This belief set an atmosphere where people were willing to accept a national bank.

The U.S. Federal Reserve got its start on Jekyll Island in 1910, then a privately owned island off the coast of Georgia. The small group of powerful bankers present at the meeting represented influential banks worldwide. Those American institutions included the J.P. Morgan companies, the banking conglomerate of William Rockefeller and Kuhn, Loeb, and Company, the Rothschild banks of England and France, and the

CHAPTER 6: FEDERAL RESERVE

Warburg banking consortium of Germany and the Netherlands. This group represented a financial trust (competitors that cooperate) that controlled approximately ¼ of the world's wealth. The bankers presented their cartel arrangement to Congress after putting the term Act on the document. With the support of President Woodrow Wilson, Congress passed the Federal Reserve Act a few days before Christmas in December of 1913. Thus, the United States became a part of the international banking cartel. *The Creature from Jekyll Island* by G. Edward Griffin tells the story.

Before 1913, the people had veto power over deficit spending because they could choose not to purchase government bonds to fund this program. With the Federal Reserve Act, the government could now sell bonds to the Fed without restraint, thus negating the people's veto power over government spending. Now the borrowers, the people, become servants to the lenders, the central bankers. Creditors will always direct the affairs of a nation.

MONETARY POLICIES

Monetary policies are the policies of the Federal Reserve to regulate the nation's money supply. If we have an inflation problem, the Fed will raise the cost of borrowing money, and if we have unemployment, the Fed will make it easier for people to borrow money. Except for the federal funds and the prime interest rate, the Fed cannot control interest rates; it can only influence interest rates. Monetary authorities are primarily academics who make decisions based on their econometric models. If events do not fit their models, they tend to ignore them.

CHAPTER 6: FEDERAL RESERVE

We have a fractional reserve banking system in the United States, meaning that banks are required to keep a fraction of their assets in reserve. Banks lend money from their excess funds. The Fed influences a bank's liquidity by encouraging an increase or a decrease in banks' excess reserves by raising or lowering the bank's required reserves. The greater the excess reserves, the higher the bank's liquidity and the more money it can lend or invest in the markets. When interest rates are near zero, the Fed can no longer lower interest rates (unless for negative interest rates), making monetary policy ineffective. As a result, there are reasons during recessionary times that people may not borrow, despite the bank's efforts to lend more money. Keynes called this a liquidity trap.

POLICY CHANGES BY THE FED

There have been significant changes in Fed policies since the financial collapse of 2007-2008. First, Congress granted the Fed permission to pay interest on a bank's reserves, which is problematic because it discourages public offerings. Faced with a choice of making loans to the public or collecting risk-free interest from the Federal Reserve, banks often chose the risk-free option. Second, since the financial collapse of 2007-2008, the Fed now grants loans to entities other than commercial banks or the federal government. Third, the Fed has been lending money to favored businesses while refusing loans to others.

CONFLICTING POLICIES

Keynesians believe that the Fed is necessary to manage the country's money supply, and Austrians suspect that it has

CHAPTER 6: FEDERAL RESERVE

caused booms and busts by misallocating resources. Keynesians believe that policymakers can make sound policies with accurate predictions, but for Austrians, life is unpredictable. Keynesians favor discretionary policies based on the situation, and Austrians believe in clearly defined rules. Keynesians believe that low interest rates will encourage more borrowing and, therefore, increase aggregate demand. Austrians are more concerned that the low-interest rates will adversely impact savings and that market forces should determine interest rates. Keynesians are satisfied with the status quo. Austrians favor government control over banking.

QUANTITATIVE EASING

The federal government borrows money by selling securities and bonds to the Federal Reserve, and the Fed credits the federal government's account by pushing a few keys on its computer. Economists call this practice monetizing the debt or quantitative easing (QE). Notice what is happening here. The Federal Reserve creates money out of thin air and then lends it out and collects interest on this newly created money—and who ultimately pays this interest? The American taxpayer! Quantitative Easing has found widespread use since 2008. Central banks, such as the Federal Reserve, Bank of Japan, and the European Central Bank, have resorted to this policy to kick-start economic growth. In the United States, we have experienced four rounds of quantitative Easing; in the fourth round, the Fed bought long-term U.S. Treasury notes, buying $85 billion in Treasuries from member banks each month. The Fed has also been active in buying mortgage-backed securities from Fannie Mae and Freddie Mac. Naturally, when the Fed increases the

CHAPTER 6: FEDERAL RESERVE

money supply more than the economy increases goods and services, we should experience an inflation problem. However, despite this flood of newly created money, inflation was kept low for a time.

The first reason QE did not cause inflation is that much of this new money flowed to other countries instead of circulating in America. Because the U.S. dollar is still the world's standard currency, there is a demand for it internationally. Second, when banks do not lend this money to the public, the funds will not cause inflation. Because the Federal Reserve pays interest on money that banks deposit at the Fed, banks have an incentive to park money at the Fed rather than lending it to people. The Fed's interest is only about .05 percent, but banks still earn substantial interest because they deposit trillions of dollars annually. Third, a sluggish economy can impede borrowing, causing a slow down in the velocity of money. Velocity measures the speed at which a dollar changes hands from person to person. A decrease in velocity can inhibit inflation despite the increase in the quantity of money in circulation. Fourth, the banks have paid out $250 billion-plus in penalties to the federal government in recent years. This money does not circulate because the government uses it to pay interest in foreigners' national debt. Finally, Austrians believe quantitative easing creates unpredictability as traders speculate whether the Fed will intervene again. By replacing the large decentralized markets with centralized control by few officials, the Fed is distorting the free market.

CANTILLION EFFECT

Artificially low interest rates tend to channel money to the safest, most credit worthy, and/or favored borrowers, which

CHAPTER 6: FEDERAL RESERVE

are seldom the best job creators. Economists call this the Cantillion Effect. In our modern economy, the Cantillon Effect is at play with a stratified socioeconomic impact, favoring investors over wage-earners. Cantillon's original thesis outlines how rising prices affect different sectors at different times and suggests that time difference effectively acts as a taxing mechanism. Modern Monetary Theory (easy money policies) favors investors over wage earners because the monied class has preference in the loanable funds market, the market where people lend and borrow money, and wage earners get the dregs. The artificially low-interest rates favor the rich over the poor, the asset class over the wage earner. The Cantillon Effect illustrates how the uneven distribution of wealth in society grows ever more uneven with low-interest rates. While the low-interest rates favor investors, the average income person receives less interest income on their savings.

AUSTRIANS

Austrians believe that quantitative easing leads to malinvestments, which only occur with artificially low-interest rates. Once a market correction takes place and price signals normalize, these investments falter. The easy credit leads to a boom, and the correction leads to a bust. In the 1940s, Ludwig von Mises and Friedrich Hayek warned us about the ill effect of easy credit. Hayek won the Nobel Prize in economics in 1974 for his work on this boom and bust theory of easy credit. His work showed that artificially low-interest rates and excessive credit creation result in a volatile imbalance between saving and investing as the easy credit blurs price signals.

CHAPTER 6: FEDERAL RESERVE

The Fed's expansionary monetary policy can hurt foreign nations. When the Fed creates money, dollars increase globally. The increase in dollars tends to reduce the dollar's value and, in essence, raises the value of other currencies. For example, when the value of the Brazil Real increases relative to the American Dollar, Brazilian products become more expensive for non-Brazilians, which inhibits Brazilian exports. Austrians point out that America is not alone in the practice of quantitative easing. Quantitative easing has trapped central banks in Japan and Europe in the same loop as the United States. Central banks believe that zero interest rates stimulate the economy and combat deflationary pressures. Despite their efforts of QE, however, median incomes along with prices and growth remain sluggish.

After years of sitting on the sidelines, the European Central Bank (ECB) has joined the fray and has engaged in its QE policy. These expansionary monetary policies usually weaken a country's exchange rate, which boosts exports. Austrians generally see quantitative easing, and the ECB bond-buying program is mainly a problem if it gives Europe an excuse to avoid reforms.

FED POLICIES BASED ON RULES

The economic pie will continue to shrink unless there is an increase in after-tax profits of small businesses and new businesses. Presently, the Fed decides what policies to implement on an ad-hoc basis; it makes decisions based on whatever feels good at the time. Austrians favor a rule-based approach. For example, if the economy grows by 2 percent, the Fed should increase the money supply by 2 percent. Conversely, if the

CHAPTER 6: FEDERAL RESERVE

economy shrinks by 2 percent, the Fed should decrease the money supply by 2 percent.

GLASS-STEAGALL & VOLCKER RULE

Under Glass-Steagall, the government regulated commercial banks, but not investment banks. Banks who used depositors' money to make risky investments aggravated the Depression of the 1930s. Many of these investments soured as the Depression progressed and made the downturn worse. Congress passed the Glass-Steagall Act in 1933 calling for the separation of commercial and investment banking; the act was only 37 pages long. Commercial banks used depositors' money to make loans, whereas investment banks used funds from wealthy individuals. Under Glass-Steagall, the government did not regulate investment banks, giving them licenses to take sizeable risks. The lack of regulation suited rich people because risky investments are more fun and potentially more profitable than safe investments. The government did regulate commercial banks to protect depositors.

In the 1990s, investment banks made enormous profits in activities that the Glass-Steagall Act made unlawful for commercial banks, and commercial banks wanted to share in the bounty. The lobbying efforts of the investment community succeeded in convincing Congress to repeal the Glass-Steagall Act with the Financial Services Modernization Act of 1999. The Financial Services Modernization Act allows banks to compete with investment banks in these risky ventures.

As part of the Dodd-Frank Wall Street Reform and Consumer Protection Act, the Volcker Rule prohibits proprietary

CHAPTER 6: FEDERAL RESERVE

trading by banking entities—in effect, reintroducing a significant portion of the Glass-Steagall Act's static divide between banks and security firms. Proprietary trading occurs when a company trades stocks, bonds, currencies, commodities, or other financial instruments with the firm's money instead of customers' money, making a profit for itself. The Volcker Rule is 77 pages long with another 882 pages of explanation.

Keynesians tend to support the Dodd-Frank Law and the Volcker Rule, whereas Austrians do not. Austrian economists believe that the Dodd-Frank Law encourages rent-seeking because businesses can sway regulators and gain favorable treatment. In the fog of uncertainty, business interests will always trump noble intentions. Regulators are usually the last ones to predict transgressions. Small banks cannot afford the compliance costs of the Dodd-Frank Law. Suppose you understand the basics behind the Glass-Steagall Act of 1933 and the Dodd-Frank Wall Street Reform and Consumer Protection Act of 2010. In that case, you get a glimpse of the differing philosophies between Keynesians and Austrians. The Glass-Steagall Act was simple because it distinguished commercial banks and investment banks and required little government involvement. In contrast, the Volcker Rule attempts to micromanage banks and is rife with confusing regulations.

Austrians believe that the Volcker Rule inhibits banks' ability to function and restricts how banks invest taxpayer-insured deposits. The Volcker Rule is a federal regulation that prohibits banks from conducting certain investment activities with their accounts. In addition, it limits their ownership of and relationship with hedge funds and private equity funds, also

CHAPTER 6: FEDERAL RESERVE

called covered funds. Under the Obama Administration, Congress worded the Volcker Rule so that its interpretation is up to the authorities.

TROUBLED ASSET RELIEF PROGRAM

The repeal of the Glass-Steagall Act in 1999 encouraged banks to take excessive risks, paving the way to the financial collapse of 2007-2008. On September 18, 2008, Treasury Secretary Henry Paulson and Fed Chairman Ben Bernanke met with legislators to propose a $700 billion bailout for banks. Paulson reportedly told Congress, If you do not do this, we might not have an economy on Monday!" As a result, the Emergency Economic Stabilization Act, which implemented the Troubled Asset Relief Program (TARP), became law on October 3, 2008. Although the bulk of the money went to the nation's largest financial institutions, authorities used some of it to bail out the automobile, insurance, and housing companies.

Neil Barofsky became the first special inspector general overseeing the Troubled Asset Relief Program (TARP). In his book, *Bailout: An Inside Account of How Washington Abandoned Main Street While Rescuing Wall Street*, he writes about his experiences in Washington D.C. and reveals how the system blocked him at every turn. He explains how the government shuffled more than $700 billion out the door with almost no oversight. Much of the money went for bonuses to elite bankers, the same bankers who contributed to the collapse.

Businesses should be profit-seeking institutions, but after receiving bailouts, they became servants of political masters who care little about profits. Politicians tend to view corporations as

CHAPTER 6: FEDERAL RESERVE

social institutions meant to achieve social outcomes that are frequently at odds with making profits. Once the government gives money to big corporations and financial institutions, they are rarely held accountable for their money. After TARP, there grew one set of rules for elite bankers and favored big businesses and another set of rules for everyone else. The Department of Justice has admitted not prosecuting bankers for fear that mass prosecution would undermine the banking industry.

CHAPTER 7: GOVERNMENT

Since the 1930's, we have gone down the rabbit hole of an ever-larger federal government, experienced the concentration of corporate power, and witnessed the ascendance of international organizations that threaten our freedom and independence. Milton Friedman warned us against tyranny in his book *Capitalism and Freedom* when he said that freedom is weak and fragile, not strong and enduring. The concentration of power is the greatest threat to our freedom. To quote Lord Acton *"Power corrupts and absolute power corrupts absolutely."* Societies that put equality and fairness as top priorities end up with neither equality nor fairness.

PRESIDENTIAL POWERS

The President can sign or veto legislation, command the armed forces, convene or adjourn Congress, grant reprieves, pardons, receive ambassadors, and make treaties with foreign governments—but the Senate needs to ratify these actions a two-thirds majority. The President may also appoint some judges with the advice and consent of the U.S. Senate. The Office of Management and Budget is to assist the President with preparing the national budget. Within the executive branch itself, the President has broad powers to manage government priorities. The president can issue rules, regulations, and instructions called executive orders, which have the binding force of law but do not require the approval of Congress. Executive orders are subject to judicial review and interpretation. Executive orders can cloud the distinction between the president and Congress because all legislative powers reside in Congress. The Executive Branch has the responsibility to execute the laws passed by Congress. When Congress presents him with a bill, he can sign it into law within ten days, or he can return it to Congress suggesting changes. Unlike many state governors, the president must approve the entire bill or reject it because, in 1996, the Supreme Court disallowed presidential line-item veto power.

MARKET FAILURE

Free markets are efficient, but even Austrians believe that they cannot provide us with everything we need because of market failure, especially since the world is imperfect. All societies need a strong central government to:

- enforce contracts between people.
- safeguard private property.
- provide a strong national defense.
- provide public goods like roads and schools.
- protect us against social costs like pollution.
- encourage merit goods that are good for us.
- help poor and disadvantaged people.

CHAPTER 7: GOVERNMENT

- establish and enforce rules to maintain order.
- promote competition and prevent monopolies.
- promote a fair distribution of income.
- promote full employment and stable prices.

ENVIRONMENT vs. GROWTH

Society must limit social costs, but who is responsible—states or the federal government? Texas has sued the federal government, challenging its ability to take over the state's air pollution authority. Texas claims the government is impeding its legal rights and has asserted that the Environmental Protection Agency's (EPA's) actions violate the Clean Air Act. Presently the federal government requires power plants to obtain greenhouse-gas permits from the federal government (instead of the state) before building new facilities or modifying existing ones.

There is a tradeoff between a clean environment and growth. For example, policies under President Obama neglected development when the EPA required power plants to install maximum achievable control technology to reduce mercury emissions and other trace gasses, forcing many coal-fired plants to shut down. There is no right or wrong here—but it is a choice society has to make—and choices always come with opportunity costs. An opportunity cost is giving up on the best option when you make a decision. For every unit of gain toward a cleaner environment, the opportunity cost increases by a multiple as we get closer to a perfectly clean environment.

CHAPTER 7: GOVERNMENT

American farmers have diverted 40 percent of corn production from food to fuel. Yet, the National Academy of Sciences claims that ethanol production increases greenhouse gas emissions and raises food prices worldwide. The National Association of Clean Air is another agency that believes that the burning of higher ethanol blends causes increased emissions of nitrogen oxides and other harmful pollutants. So why is the EPA supporting ethanol? One reason is that the ethanol industry has significant political influence. Another reason is that the EPA administrator has dictatorial powers, and he can issue mandates without Senate approval.

The Paris Agreement's central aim is to strengthen the global response to the threat of climate change by keeping a global temperature rise this century well below 2 degrees Celsius. Unfortunately, many of the 195 countries that agreed to lower planet-warming greenhouse gas emissions are not sincere, and they have ulterior motives that have nothing to do with climate change. Some countries joined because there are financial incentives, some joined because they want to be a part of a group, and some joined because there may be costs of not joining the group.

Dr. Judith Curry, Professor and former Chair of the School of Earth and Atmospheric Sciences at the Georgia Institute of Technology, delivered a speech to the U.S. Senate Commerce Committee debunking global warming. In her testimony, she stated that many scientists had become a part of groupthink, and green activists have pressured them to agree that global warming is a threat. There is evidence that Dr. Curry is correct. The Intergovernmental Panel on Climate Change reported in 2013 that the global surface temperature as measured by weather satellites had shown a much smaller increasing linear

CHAPTER 7: GOVERNMENT

trend over the past 15 years than over the past 30 to 60 years. The evidence that the earth has not experienced an increase in global warming over the past 15 years has caused many green movements to claim that we are in a pause or a global warming hiatus.

DETAILED LAWS

Congress established the federal income tax system in 1913 under President Woodrow Wilson. The original law was one page. Today it is more than 72,000 pages. In the same year, Congress passed the Federal Reserve Act. Authorities can only interpret complicated and lengthy laws because no one can understand the whole of them. A favorite gambit for Congress is to make the laws so long and convoluted that only the big players will have the resources to comply. These added costs make American companies less competitive around the world. For example, a flat rate tax system, whereby almost everyone pays the same rate regardless of income, would be much simpler and more efficient than our present system, but it would leave little room for politics. Consider the Federal Work Opportunity Tax Credit, which typically lowers a company's taxes by thousands of dollars per employee. This tax credit frequently goes unclaimed because it takes extensive time and paperwork for each worker. Another targeted break, the tax deduction for energy-efficient buildings, often requires computer modeling costing as much as $50,000, convincing many business owners not to take the credit. Many companies say it is too complicated to claim tax breaks, and the ones who try can find themselves at odds with the Internal Revenue Service.

CHAPTER 7: GOVERNMENT

THE RULE OF LAW IS JEOPARDIZED

When the Senate refused to confirm President Obama's picks for the National Labor Relations Board (NLRB), he proclaimed the Senate to be in recess and appointed the members anyway. This action made a mockery of that chamber's advice-and-consent role. When Obama disagreed with federal laws criminalizing the use of medical marijuana, he instructed the Justice Department not to prosecute transgressors. The bailout of automobile companies turned contract law on its head when the Obama White House subordinated the bondholders' rights to those of its union allies, contrary to bankruptcy laws.

The government can imprison people for killing bald eagles, yet companies that produce wind power are exempt from the law. Congress passed Obamacare, yet declared it invalid for members of Congress and their staff. The Environmental Protection Agency issued new ethanol mandates on 143 refineries but exempted one lucky refinery for political reasons. The Obama Administration made multiple changes to the Affordable Care Act without Congressional consent, contrary to the Constitution.

In his book *Animal Farm*, George Orwell set out to show how power corrupts, no matter how noble the intent. A group of animals centralizes control over the farm to ensure equality. The novel ends with the barnyard commandments, high on their righteousness, reducing the commandments to only one, which is: *"All animals are equal, but some animals are more equal than others."* The book illustrates that power corrupts, and absolute power corrupts absolutely. Millionaires, healthcare providers, energy companies, political groups, and other

CHAPTER 7: GOVERNMENT

politically favored groups are the most equal. The point of the book is that as the government grows, so too will inequality.

GOVERNMENT PROGRAMS

Americans had tamed the frontier by the last quarter of the 19th century; they built cities, grew businesses, and established a country, but not all citizens shared in the wealth. The Progressive Movement highlighted the deficiencies in the economic system. The modern Progressive Movement has impacted education, health care, tax policies, and other federal programs. Members of the Democratic Party tend to be Progressives, and members of the Republican Party tend to disfavor the income redistribution policies of the Progressive Movement. In his book *Big Agenda*, David Horowitz explains how the Conservatives can stop the Democratic Party from dismantling the constitutional foundations. Horowitz believes that, rather than supporting specific programs, members of the Progressive Movement tailor their policies to fit the moment. He cites Obamacare as a prime example. He believes that the Progressives designed the program to fail to replace it with socialized medicine, a single-payer plan under government control. *The High Cost of Good Intentions*, 2017, by John Cogan is about why entitlement programs keep growing. He explains why government benefits always multiply and are nearly impossible to repeal.

SOCIAL SECURITY (SS)

The Federal Insurance Contributions Act (FICA) includes two separate taxes; Social Security and Medicare. Monthly

CHAPTER 7: GOVERNMENT

benefits depend on past earnings and retirement age. The Social Security Administration estimates that the system will begin to withdraw money from the Social Security Trust Fund in a few years. The funds will not be there because Social Security is an unfunded liability. Instead of letting the funds accumulate in the Trust Fund and earn interest, Congress used the money for general purposes and replaced it with nonnegotiable IOUs. A nonnegotiable IOU is an IOU that the public cannot buy and sell. Because social security is a pay-as-you-go system, it is the world's largest Ponzi scheme. In a Ponzi scheme, participants receive returns on their contributions from the latest contributors. Suppose that I assure you and others that I am an excellent investor and that I can triple your money in five years. Instead of investing your money in the markets as I claimed, I pay you great returns from the money I collect from new people I bring into the system. The plan begins to fall apart when there are fewer new people. Like a Ponzi scheme, Social Security relies on a constant influx of new people. Social Security is the opposite of how private insurance typically works. Insurance companies usually pay claims from the return on their principle while preserving the principle.

MEDICARE

Medicare is a four-part program that provides health insurance for people sixty-five years and older and some permanently disabled young people. The Bureau of Labor Statistics estimates that by 2030, only 2.4 workers will support one older adult. With more than 1.5 million baby boomers enrolling in Medicare annually, the program's future is one of the most critical economic issues.

CHAPTER 7: GOVERNMENT

MEDICAID

James Madison warned in the Federalist Papers about laws so voluminous that people cannot read them and so incoherent that no one can understand them. A typical provision of Medicare reads like this:

"In the case of a plan for which there are average per capita monthly savings described in section 1395w–24 (b)(3)(C) or 1395w–24 (b)(4)(C) of this title, as the case may be, the amount specified in this subparagraph is the amount of the monthly rebate computed under section 1395w–24 (b)(1)(C)(I) of this title for that plan and year (as reduced by the amount of any credit provided under section 1395w–24 (b)(1)(C)(iv) [2] of this title.

POSSIBLE SOLUTIONS

Austrians believe that long and detailed laws, like the 2,700-page health care bill and a 2,300-page financial reform bill, cause problems. Adding to the confusion is the fact that a statement can be very long and include unrelated topics. The length and complexity of such laws are why some states have given line-item veto power to their governors so that they can go through a bill line by line and veto portions of it. Congress attempted to grant this power to the president in 1996, but in 1998 the U.S. Supreme Court ruled the act to be unconstitutional in a 6-3 decision in Clinton v. The city of New York.

CHAPTER 7: GOVERNMENT

DISINCENTIVES CAN BE A PROBLEM

The Tax Foundation has published an International Tax Competitive Index. According to the foundation, the index measures the extent to which a country's tax system adheres to the two principles of tax policy—competitiveness and neutrality. A competitive tax code limits taxation on businesses and fosters investment. Tax codes that are not competitive drive investment elsewhere, leading to slower economic growth. The Tax Foundation means a tax system that seeks to raise the most revenue with the least economic distortions. According to the Tax Foundation, the United States ranks thirty-second of the thirty-four industrialized countries in the Organization for Economic Co-operation and Development (OECD) for tax neutrality. Tax neutrality is characteristic wherein taxes do not interfere with the natural flow of capital toward its most productive use. According to the Tax Foundation, America's tax system is at odds with tax neutrality.

UNFUNDED LIABILITIES

Unfunded liabilities occur when the government commits itself to spend money on programs but does not make adequate provisions for funding the program into the future. Therefore, the government is incurring liability without proper funding. Were the government confiscating the total adjusted gross income of American taxpayers and corporate taxable income, it would not be enough to balance the budget. Balancing the budget means that the government spends only the money it receives. David M Walker, a former comptroller general, says that the country's dysfunctional democracy prevents a return to fiscal sanity. He has been warning people of a collapse. He believes we have a

CHAPTER 7: GOVERNMENT

long-term structural deficit problem because of unfunded liabilities.

THE NATIONAL BUDGET

Off-budget spending makes it difficult to access government spending from one year to the next. Off-budget spending is spending that Congress does not count as part of the regular budget, and therefore it does not appear in official records. Off-budget spending, in short, is a tool used to conceal the cost of government programs. Two off-budget entities are Social Security and the Postal Service. Off-budget spending is not a part of the federal budget. The U. S. Postal Service has lost millions of dollars in a day, so the Senate allocates additional dollars but delays reforms that would save money. Postal Service management, to its credit, has a credible plan to put the agency on a firmer financial footing. The Post Office has closed about half of its mail processing centers and thousands of post offices—letting local stores do the heavy lifting. However, the Senate continues to throw up one obstacle after another, preventing further policy changes. Washington Speak camouflages government spending. For example, if I spend $100 in year one and $200 in year two, I would say that I spent 100% more in year two than in year one. Washington calculates spending differently. If Congress spends $100 in year one and says that it plans to spend $200 in year two but instead spends $150 in year two, it claims it cut spending by $50!

CHAPTER 8:
FISCAL POLICIES

There are two macroeconomic problems, inflation and unemployment, and there are two categories of solutions, monetary and fiscal policies. Monetary policies are policies of the Federal Reserve, and fiscal policies are policies of the federal government. Pro-cyclical policies accentuate the business cycle—counter-cyclical policies moderate the process. The Fed will increase the money supply with unemployment and decrease it with inflation. Since the financial collapse of 2007-2008, the Fed has kept interest rates below market rates. Monetary policies are better at fighting inflation than unemployment. The Fed can always decrease the money supply to lower aggregate demand, but it cannot always increase the money supply. Unemployed people, or people who fear unemployment, will not borrow money just because of low interest rates.

The government will use its fiscal policies to adjust spending, borrowing, taxes, and others to stimulate demand when unemployment is a problem. The government rarely uses budgetary policies to fight inflation because any cut in spending hurts a particular interest group. In addition, most government spending goes to entitlement programs, making fiscal policies

CHAPTER 8: FISCAL POLICIES

somewhat ineffective. Balancing the budget is of less concern to Keynesians than to Austrians because Keynesians have embraced the idea of functional finance. Functional finance is the philosophy of aiming fiscal policy at achieving potential GDP regardless of what those policies do to the national debt or anything else. Austrians favor market forces as opposed to demand management economics.

AUSTRIANS

Austrians believe in Say's Law in a free market economy with ample competition. That is, supply creates its demand. Because suppliers paid wages, demand will be sufficient to sustain full employment. Of course, there may be unemployment at times because of a mismatch between wants and supplies, leakages, and natural disasters, but a free market economy will tend toward full employment. Leakages are monies that leave the income stream. Leakages occur when citizens pay taxes, import goods, and save. Injections are monies that enter the income stream, such as government spending, exports, and lending. Austrians believe that planned leakages equal planned injections over the long run and that ultimately unemployment is voluntary.

A good book written on the subject of the depression of 1921 is *The Forgotten Depression, 2014,* by James Grant. Mr. Grant argues that the government addressed the severe downturn in the American economy in 1920-21 with a policy of nonintervention. As unemployment increased, President Harding refused to take action, preferring to let prices and wages continue to fall. Rather than increased activism, he called for a smaller government. By late 1921, commodity prices and economic activity reversed their decline and started to rise. Most educators

CHAPTER 8: FISCAL POLICIES

believe that the laissez-faire policies of President Hoover in the early 1930s aggravated unemployment, and Roosevelt saved American capitalism with his New Deal Programs after 1933. Austrians believe that the policies of the New Deal hampered recovery. The book *Meltdown*, by Thomas Woods Jr., 2009, is a compelling read on the subject.

President Herbert Hoover favored active fiscal policies by launching public works projects, raising taxes, and extending emergency loans to failing firms. He lent money to states for relief programs and encouraged businesses to raise wages. In the presidential election of 1932, Roosevelt blamed the Hoover Administration for too much spending and intervention. Nevertheless, when FDR took office in 1933, he expanded programs by raising taxes, established public works and social welfare programs, and encouraged investments by keeping prices as high as possible. Austrians believe that the Hoover-Roosevelt policies prevented the economy from seeking its full-employment equilibrium. Austrians believe that the economic recovery would have come sooner had the government not intervened.

KEYNES and the GREAT DEPRESSION

In his book, *The General Theory of Employment, Interest, and Money*, 1936, John Maynard Keynes argued the Austrian viewpoint was valid in the particular case but not in the general case. Thus, he included the word general in the title. Because Keynes believed the economy was tending toward a less than full employment equilibrium in the 1930s, he favored managing demand to shift the economy to a full-employment equilibrium. His remedy was to sell government securities (bonds) and

CHAPTER 8: FISCAL POLICIES

increase government spending. Notice that the goal is not just full employment. The goal is to position the economy so that it is tending toward full employment. According to Keynes, once the economy is in full-employment equilibrium, there is little need for stimulus policies. Politicians, however, liked the idea of discretionary spending so much that they have overdosed on the concept. If Keynes were alive today, he probably would not be a Keynesian.

THE EMPLOYMENT ACT OF 1946

The Employment Act of 1946 gave the government the responsibility of promoting maximum employment, production, and purchasing power. The president was required to submit an annual report to Congress stating current employment levels, production and purchasing power, and his goals to achieve full employment.

KEYNESIANS

Keynesians believe that fiscal policies can avoid a liquidity trap, take advantage of the balanced budget multiplier, and prevent the paradox of thrift. A liquidity trap occurs when too much money is trapped in banks despite low-interest rates—causing an interruption in the circular flow of money and worsening unemployment. Banks are the heart of the economy—money comes in, and money goes out. The economy slows when the supply of money circulating is insufficient to maintain full employment.

If consumers and investors do not borrow enough money, when there is a liquidity trap, the only solution is for the

CHAPTER 8: FISCAL POLICIES

government to prime the pump by borrowing and spending. On this, Austrians and Keynesians agree. Keynesians justify deficit spending because of the balanced budget multiplier. The government balances the budget when it spends what it takes in through taxes, no more, no less. The balanced budget multiplier recognizes that consumers will save a portion of their income, whereas the government does not. Therefore, dollars in the hands of the government boost the multiplier effect. Keynesians also use the balanced budget multiplier to justify higher taxes.

Austrians believe that savings and investing are sources of growth. Austrians believe that the economy will recover from depression independently as long as government policies do not hamper the self-adjusting mechanisms. Austrians believe that savings and investing are sources of growth and that too much government borrowing and spending can be counterproductive. Austrians tend to disfavor discretionary fiscal policies but favor automatic stabilizers and monetary policies. An automatic stabilizer, like unemployment benefits, is a policy that goes into effect automatically.

Keynesians justify deficit spending because of the paradox of thrift. Bernard Mandeville first presented the paradox in 1714 with his publication of *The Fable of the Bees*. The paradox states that if everyone tries to save more, aggregate demand will insufficient to support full employment. The paradox of thrift promotes spending over thriftiness because significant increases in saving can be a drag on demand. Austrians disagree and support policies that encourage savings. The more people save—the more banks can lend. When banks inject money into the economy, the economy grows as consumption and investments increase.

CHAPTER 8: FISCAL POLICIES

RENT-SEEKING

Washington, D.C. has about 18,000 lobbyists who pander to members of Congress; they represent about 12,000 clients who spent $2.5 billion in a recent year. An additional 10,000 unregistered lobbyists work outside Washington, D.C. You can find who these lobbyists are, who their clients are, and how much money they spend seeking favors from Congress at http://www.opensecrets.org/lobby/.

FISCAL POLICIES AND UNIONS

There has been a decline in private unions (unions that bargain with businesses) but an increase in public unions (unions that bargain with governments). Private unions have limited power because firms need to make a profit. Public unions have more bargaining power because the government does not have to profit, and politicians can raise taxes to pay for union benefits. Because of this, state laws hold private and public unions to different standards, placing more restrictions on public unions than on private unions.

AUSTRIANS AND FISCAL POLICIES

Draw a line and label it security floor. This line represents a financial level by which the government will not allow most people to fall. Draw another line above this and mark its success ceiling. Where does the money come from to maintain the security floor? It has to come from the top. When the security floor rises too much, growth diminishes as the success ceiling falls. Austrians believe that if we had a king who had absolute power, who possessed all knowledge, and always made the right

CHAPTER 8: FISCAL POLICIES

decisions, then discretionary fiscal policies would work. However, we live in a democracy with 535 members of Congress who have imperfect knowledge and who are motivated by politics and not economics.

LAFFER CURVE

What effect will a tax increase have on government revenue? The answer depends on where the economy is on the Laffer Curve. When the government increases taxes starting from zero, government revenues will increase because citizens will see the benefits and not experience much pain. However, government revenues will decrease beyond a certain level because the incentives to work, save, and invest diminish. In addition, beyond a certain level, people will avoid taxes by legal or illegal means; they will escape to other countries, work less, cheat, or go underground, resulting in less revenue for the government.

TAXES

The government foresaw a collection problem in 1942 when it doubled income taxes. In those days, taxpayers mailed their annual tax payments directly to Washington. However, as spring arrived in 1943, Henry Morgenthau, the Treasury secretary, was concerned about tax evasion. Now meet Beardsley Ruml, a man of ideas who observed that people preferred installment payments. So instead of paying their annual taxes all at once, the government could make businesses collect taxes from each paycheck and forward the funds directly to Washington. No longer would the employee have to face his tax bill square in the eye.

CHAPTER 8: FISCAL POLICIES

PERSONAL TAXES

Congress passed the most sweeping tax code overhaul in decades which went into effect in January of 2018. The law keeps seven tax brackets but changes the tax rates, shifting income into lower tax brackets. Studies by the Tax Foundation and the Tax Policy Center indicate that most taxpayers will pay less under the new rules. You are taxed based on your taxable income, which is your gross income minus deductions. The most sweeping change is doubling the standard deduction $6,350 to $12,000 for single filers and from $12,700 to $24,000 for married filers. If your deductions are less than the standard deduction, you claim the standard deduction. Any take away from your gross income lowers your taxable income, and you pay less in taxes.

The law simplifies taxes because it reduces or eliminates itemized deductions in favor of the standard deduction. The law limits the deduction for state and local income taxes, property taxes, and real estate taxes to $10,000 and increases the child tax credit to $2,000 from $1,000. Tax credits are better than tax deductions because credits reduce your taxes dollar-for-dollar, while deductions only lower your taxable income. If you buy a home between now and 2026, you can deduct the interest of up to $750,000. The new legislation wiped out the deduction for home equity debt, including existing loans, beginning in 2018. By 2019, only medical expenses that exceed 10% of adjusted gross income are deductible. The new law preserves all the most charitable donation deductions, but fewer people will claim this deduction because of the higher standard deduction.

If you are in a high-income household in a high-tax state with a mortgage and high property taxes, these changes could end

CHAPTER 8: FISCAL POLICIES

up increasing your tax liability. However, if you do not itemize your deductions, these changes will not be an issue, and the increased standard deduction should benefit you. About 70% of taxpayers claim the standard deduction, so most taxpayers claiming this deduction likely will help. In addition, if you are a low or middle-income household, the standard deduction combined with an increased child tax credit should lower your tax bill.

CORPORATE TAXES

The new tax law reduces the corporate tax rate to a flat 21% from the highest 35% rate in the prior system. Lowering the corporate tax rate will increase the profits of many companies, providing additional capital for business expansion, increasing dividends to shareholders, and making the U.S. a more attractive place for foreign businesses to open operations.

CHAPTER 9: PRICES

The Bureau of Labor Statistics defines inflation as a pervasive and general rise in the average price level. Inflation is always a monetary phenomenon—when the money supply increases more than goods and services increase, we experience inflation. The three factors that influence prices are the velocity of money (V), the quantity of money (M), and the size of our GDP (Q), therefore P = MV/Q.

WHOM DOES INFLATION HURT?

Inflation hurts persons with fixed incomes the most and flexible the least. The elderly tend to have fixed incomes, whereas the young can adjust. Savers lose if prices exceed the interest rate and lenders gain. Negative real returns will encourage savers to take money out of savings and invest in the stock market or other risky ventures.

There is nothing wrong with a slow and steady rise in prices, especially when people correctly anticipate a price increase. Inflation that is high and erratic, however, can cause havoc for almost everyone. Any sudden and pronounced change in prices, either up or down, can cause problems. It would help if

CHAPTER 9: PRICES

you did not confuse inflation with the price mechanism where prices change in response to market forces.

The rule of 72 will give you an idea of the impact of inflation over time. Take any incremental increase and divide the number into 72, and you will get an approximation of how long it will take prices to double. For example, if the inflation rate is 2% each year, it will take about 36 years for prices to double (72/2=36). If the inflation rate is 4%, it will take about 18 years to double (72/4=18).

BRIEF HISTORY

Rome got into trouble between 218 A.D. and 268 A.D. when the government financed a large army, embarked on expensive public works projects, and raised taxes. Entrepreneurship fell off, and tax evasion increased. The government increased coins in circulation and debased the currency by replacing gold and silver coins with cheaper metal. Diocletian blamed merchants for the inflation problem, and in 301 A.D., he attempted a price freeze. His edict led to shortages and hoarding, which led to penalties against hoarding. These and other policies depressed the economy and made citizens wards of the state.

When Germany entered the First World War in 1914, it opted to finance the war by borrowing money instead of raising taxes. After the war, Germany increased the money supply to reduce the mark's value to encourage exports. Germany's actions culminated in a classic currency war among the world's economies. Prices rose more than fivefold each week from July to November of 1923. By 1924, inflation had radically

CHAPTER 9: PRICES

redistributed the wealth of Germany, hitting the middle class the hardest. The poor had little money to lose while the rich transferred theirs into forms not affected by inflation, such as deposits in foreign banks, precious metals, and land.

Zimbabwe experienced hyperinflation in 2006 when the price of a single sheet of toilet paper was $417 in Zimbabwean dollars, and a roll was $145,750. Public school fees and other ever-rising government surcharges exceeded the monthly incomes of many urban families lucky enough to find work. In 2006, the government printed trillions of new Zimbabwean dollars to keep ministries functioning and shield key supporters' salaries.

BRETTON WOODS SYSTEM

World War II had a devastating effect on the global monetary system. A plan for restoring order came in 1944 at Bretton Woods, New Hampshire, with a meeting of 730 delegates from 44 Allied nations. Of paramount concern was replacing the British currency as the standard for settling international transactions. High gold reserves in America made the U.S. dollar a natural replacement. Because all nations pegged their currencies to gold at predetermined rates, all countries knew the value of their money relative to gold. The U.S. dollar became the standard currency because the U.S. guaranteed gold in return for dollars upon demand.

This fixed international exchange rate system did not last because of the inflationary 1970s. It was not so much inflation as it was the different inflation rates. If America experiences a 10 percent inflation rate, the value of the dollar declines by 10

CHAPTER 9: PRICES

percent. If England has a 15 percent inflation rate, the English pound drops in value by 15 percent. With values changing relative to one another, how can countries trade if they assume fixed exchange rates?

From 1963 to 1969, President Lyndon Johnson increased spending on the Vietnam War and Medicaid and Medicare as part of his War on Poverty. America's inflation problem began in 1969 when President Richard Nixon convinced the Fed to increase the money supply so that Congress could continue to fund the war and President Lyndon Johnson's Great Society welfare programs. Inflation reared its ugly head because of this increase in the money supply.

President Nixon imposed wage-price controls in 1971, ran budget deficits, and announced he was a Keynesian. The Nixon deficits caused foreigners to flee the dollar for other currencies as they lost faith in the U.S. economy. And on August 15, 1971, President Nixon told a national television audience that the gold standard was kaput. After this, the United States refused to value the dollar at 1/35th of an ounce of gold and closed the gold window. Before President Nixon severed the ties between the dollar and gold, the Federal Reserve could not create money as it does today.

With the closing of the gold window, nations could no longer demand payment of gold in return for U.S. dollars. Governments replaced the fixed-rate system with a freely flexible approach where the market-determined values. At this point, many countries lost confidence in the U.S. economy because of Washington's prolific social programs and chronic deficit spending. As governments abandoned the U.S. dollar,

CHAPTER 9: PRICES

Washington looked for ways to reinvigorate demand for the dollar leading to the Petrodollar System.

CREDIT CREATION and GROWTH

A new economic model took shape in 1971. Instead of countries seeking growth policies, growth took a back seat to credit creation and consumption. There is a grave danger that this credit-fueled economic paradigm will break down. In his book, *The New Depression*, Richard Duncan explains that we have creditism and not capitalism. Creditism has created extraordinarily rapid growth for decades, but it has hit its limit to produce more change because we pay our national debts by making money. Creating new money is like a person taking drugs. A drug addict may feel good for a while, but eventually, the craving returns, except when it takes higher doses to attain the same feeling when no amount of drugs can bring back that feel-good state. At this point, the only cure is an agonizing and painful withdrawal process. Likewise, at some point, quantitative easing will be ineffective, and America will experience withdrawal symptoms.

FIAT CURRENCIES

When nations replace sound money with fiat currencies, inflation is never far behind. Under the gold standard, we could not increase the money supply unless we increased the quantity of gold. Under a fiat system, there is no limit to money creation. In Karl Fenninger's book, *Leverage – How Cheap Money Will Destroy the World*, he shows how money creation will destroy economies. The world's major countries have gone from

CHAPTER 9: PRICES

capitalistic systems to crony capitalism, where powerful interests control the levers of government policy. Instead of slow and steady growth, the rich and powerful engineer economic bubbles so that they can take advantage of the swings. Special interest groups profit as the economy zooms upward, and the government protects them from losses when the economy tanks.

THE VALUE OF MONEY

The politicizing of national currencies has spawned alternative forms of money, for example, Bitcoin. Bitcoin is a cryptocurrency created in 2009 by a person using the alias Satoshi Nakamoto. Ethereum is another virtual currency that is gaining popularity. People can use these virtual currencies for transactions without banks or government — they only exist as ones and zeroes on computers.

The politicizing of national currencies has spawned alternative forms of money. A blockchain system maintains the value of virtual currencies, like Bitcoin, because a set of rules determine how many Bitcoins come into existence at any point in time. The system pays miners who succeed in solving mathematical problems with new Bitcoins. The amount of electricity it takes to run the mining computers is so expensive that miners seek locations with inexpensive renewable energy. Iceland is expected to use more energy mining virtual currencies than it uses to power its homes. Chelan County in Washington State uses more electricity for miners than it uses in its 50 hospitals. Once miners win the bitcoins, they store them in a digital wallet. Japan has declared Bitcoin as legal tender.

CHAPTER 9: PRICES

There is demand for the U.S. dollar, but the supply is unlimited, and there you have the difference. If a well-defined set of rules limit the number of circulating dollars, then virtual currencies would be unnecessary. Virtual currencies are likely to succeed so long as the value of government currencies rests on politics and special interests.

If bitcoin were the only virtual currency, the quantity would be constrained. Still, because there are several virtual currencies on the market, this unlimited availability compromises the advantage of virtual currencies. The fact that virtual currencies are dependent on computers is another problem. Any number of things can happen that would shut down the whole system. Bitcoin is open-source and copyright-free and is accessible to everyone; its backbone is a blockchain program—a public ledger on the internet of all Bitcoin transactions. A volunteer army of developers has made Bitcoin secure. The New York Stock Exchange (NYSE) lists a Bitcoin price index (NYXBT). NYXBT will represent the daily US dollar value of one Bitcoin at 4 pm (BST) daily. Selling digital coins online is becoming a big business. Ethereum raised $12 million in just 10 minutes in April of 2017!

A decentralized monetary system based on bits and bytes can be viable with enough support. Physical currencies represent a shared standard of value by keeping track of who owes whom—virtual currencies can do the same. Society determines the economic importance by the currency's usefulness and its level of scarcity. A book on virtual money is The Age of Cryptocurrency: How Bitcoin and Digital Money are Challenging the Global Economic Order, by Paul Vigna and Michael J. Casey, St. Martin's Press, 2015. In their book, the authors answer the question Why should anyone care about Bitcoin? According to

CHAPTER 9: PRICES

the authors, Bitcoin is poised to launch a revolution that could reinvent traditional financial and social structures while bringing billions of people into a new global economy. Cryptocurrency holds the promise of a system without the middleman. The digital currency world will take place because the underlying technology is here to stay. No digital currency will replace the dollar soon, but the technology will become ever more popular.

STAGFLATION

Policy reversals were common during the 1970s. When inflation is persistent and deep-rooted, it will take time before reducing the money supply will lower prices. Before prices begin to head south, the economy may experience more unemployment. Employment may improve when the Fed reverses itself and increases the money supply, but this may cause more inflation. Suppose the public demands action to bring a halt to the inflation problem. In that case, the tight monetary policy will worsen the unemployment problem, and when unemployment worsens—well, you get the idea.

Policy reversals of the 1970s resulted in stagflation, a cycle of increasing prices and unemployment. How did we get off this merry-go-round? In 1980, Paul Volcker, the Federal Reserve Chairman, decided to keep a tight rein on the money supply. Mr. Volcker became unpopular as the economy experienced a severe recession in 1980 and 1981. He refused to increase the money supply to combat unemployment, and the price level eventually subsided. Once he got a handle on the inflation problem, he concentrated on the unemployment problem. For the rest of the 1980s, with the help of President

CHAPTER 9: PRICES

Reagan's supply-side economic policies, we experienced prosperity and moderate prices.

SOLUTIONS

Productivity gains can solve our problems because lower costs will lead to lower prices. Prices would decrease with productivity gains along with stable money. However, we could experience inflation as long as the money supply increases more than goods and services increase within our national economy.

DEFLATION

Deflation is a persistent and general decline in prices. People who gain from deflation are those who are debt-free and pay for most things in cash. Creditors also benefit because they receive more highly valued dollars from debtors. Japan became the first major economy since the Great Depression to fall into extended deflation. Deflation continues in Japan, although Japan's central bank has been monetizing vast amounts of government debt for several years in the hopes of raising prices.

A slow but steady decline in prices is one thing; a sudden drop in prices is something else. With a gradual decline in prices, the economy has a chance to adjust, but when prices fall suddenly, adjustments are painful. A deflationary period will keep interest rates low. A negative interest rate would mean that you would have to pay your bank interest on your savings. Deflation and negative interest rates will act as a deterrent to savings, which is the bedrock of growth.

CHAPTER 9: PRICES

Before the financial collapse of 2007-2008, few economists would have suspected a relationship between quantitative easing and deflation. A belief among economists is that an increased money supply will cause inflation, not deflation. However, some economists now recognize that quantitative easing can lead to deflation. Because quantitative easing has kept interest rates close to zero, banks have been reluctant to lend money to the public where it could cause inflation. Instead, banks have deposited money at the Federal Reserve to earn interest, loaned it to foreigners, or made speculative investments in the Derivatives Market. Quantitative easing has encouraged an increase in speculation as investors have fled the money market searching for higher returns. Consequently, many of these investments have increased in value. Quantitative easing has thus benefitted the rich more than the poor. The Dodd-Frank Act of 2010 has codified this trend of the rich getting richer through government policies that favor one group over another. According to the law, in the event of an economic collapse, bank losses will be refinanced by creditors. When you put money in a bank, you become a creditor.

THE DEMOGRAPHIC CLIFF

According to *The Demographic Cliff: How to Survive and Prosper During the Great Deflation of 2014-2019* by Harry Dent, demographics is the ultimate indicator that allows us to see around corners to predict the most fundamental economic trends. Dent spends a good part of his book arguing that the demographic cliff has turned against the United States. Dent argues that the next big crash will bring a period of deflation. He believes that the demographics of the retiring baby boomers and

CHAPTER 9: PRICES

the smaller generation following will reduce prices. With a general collapse and the lack of job opportunities for the young generation, there will be a slowdown in economic activity, which will depress prices. At the same time, deleveraging will take place whereby people will reduce debt and sell assets. The general price level will also fall when the economic bubble bursts. Dent believes we are in a bubble brought about by excessive liquidity, too much debt, and as with all bubbles, it will explode, causing unemployment and falling prices. Most people are not concerned about deflation because they benefit from the lower prices, but deflation affects business. Consequently, These events will have an impact on markets as deflation leads to private and public insolvency.

CHAPTER 10: EMPLOYMENT

Economists like to quip that a recession occurs when your neighbor is out of work, and depression is when you are out of work! The difference between recessions and depressions is unclear, except that all economists agree that depression is worse than a recession. America has witnessed three depressions: 1837, 1893, and the Great Depression of the 1930s. Other years of high unemployment occurred in 1857, 1873, 1907, and 2007-2008. We had a downturn in 1920, but the economy quickly recovered. Quantitative easing, excessive regulations, the policies to fight so-called global warming, debt by almost everyone, and the retreat of small banks in favor of large banks will usher in the subsequent depression.

But perhaps the most profound policy affecting our lives will be the practice of bail-ins. One of the best authors on the subject is Ellen Brown. Ellen Brown is the founder of the Public Banking Institute and the author of a dozen books and hundreds of articles. Two of her books are *The Web of Debt* (2012) and *The Public Bank Solution* (2013). In The Web of Debt, she reveals how the Federal Reserve has usurped the power to create

CHAPTER 10: EMPLOYMENT

money from the people and how we can get it back. In The Public Bank Solution, she traces the evolution of public and private banking models while explaining the global banking system.

The G20 is an informal group of 19 countries and the European Union, with the International Monetary Fund and the World Bank representatives. Representatives of these groups meet once a year as a group and individually at other times during the year. The goal is to promote cooperation among members to achieve stable and sustainable growth. On the weekend of November 16, 2014, the group endorsed the Financial Stability Board's Adequacy of Loss-Absorbing Capacity of Global Systemically Important Banks in Resolution, which changed banking rules. In the event of a world, depression is it better for banks to fail, or is it better that depositors take the hit? The answer is depositors. This resolution solidifies the practice of bail-ins over the practice of bailouts or bankruptcy.

THE DERIVATIVES MARKET

One of the most significant risks to the world's financial health is the quadrillion derivatives market. It's complex, it's unregulated, and its notional value is estimated to be 20 times the size of the world economy! Derivatives are legal agreements that involve bets between parties on the outcome of some future event. Economists call these legal agreements derivatives because some event derives their value. Derivative contracts are a part of the Futures Market because the results will take place in the future. Suppose we make a bet on the weather a month from now. I say that it will rain, and you bet that it will not rain. We then draft a contract binding our agreement based on this future

CHAPTER 10: EMPLOYMENT

event. Whoever owns this piece of paper on the specified day and is on the winning side of the bet collects money from the other party. Investors enter into derivative contracts over the price of stocks, agricultural products, foreign exchange rates, or anything else.

The G20 resolution of 2014 ensures that your life savings will be wiped out in the case of a meltdown in the derivatives market. Rather than reining in the trillion-dollar derivatives market, the resolution prioritizes the payment of bank's derivatives obligations to each other ahead of everyone else. The hardest hit will be the state pension and healthcare funds because they are woefully underfunded. For example, states have almost no money saved up for future retiree healthcare costs.

Bail-ins started elsewhere, but the United States is the most vulnerable because of the Dodd-Frank Act, making derivative claimants go first when banks fail. Deposits are insured by the FDIC up to $250,000 per account, but the FDIC fund would be inadequate in a major economic meltdown. Besides, the FDIC stands in line behind derivatives and state and local bonds in the event of a collapse. So derivatives have superiority over creditors; creditors are shareholders and bondholders, but creditors are also depositors. As we move more and more toward a cashless society, it will become ever more difficult to shield your money from the clutches of your banker in the event of a banking collapse.

Before the repeal of the Glass-Steagall Act in 1999, commercial banks could not participate in the derivatives market; it was unlawful for them to put depositors' money at elevated risk. Because the repeal of the Glass-Steagall Act blurred the lines between commercial and investment banks, commercial

CHAPTER 10: EMPLOYMENT

banks now participate in the derivatives market. The catalyst that could precipitate a derivatives collapse could be the fall in oil prices. Oil companies are major derivative investors. If low oil prices lead to massive losses, the derivatives market will take a big hit. But to anticipate the future, let's look for clues in the past.

1930s GREAT DEPRESSION

What caused the unemployment rate to reach 25% in the 1930s? Producers' greed in the 1920s was a factor. Business owners believed that high prices and low wages would guarantee extravagant profits. This scheme worked for a while because of rapid growth— this was the Roaring Twenties! The low wages and high prices eventually led to insufficient demand, causing a buildup of excessive inventory and unemployment. Once business owners realize that they are producing more than they are selling and their warehouses are piling up with unsold inventory, they will cut back production and lay off workers. Risky investments accelerated the downward spiral in the 1920s as investors scrambled to protect their fortunes by taking enormous risks.

Farming compounded the problem because farmers were a large segment of the population. During World War I, farmers produced record crops and livestock to handle the increased demand. When prices fell after the war, farmers tried to grow even more to pay their debts, taxes, and living expenses. In the early 1930s, prices dropped so low that many farmers went bankrupt and lost their farms. The Fed's practice of raising interest rates after the war also hurt farmers.

CHAPTER 10: EMPLOYMENT

During World War One, the Federal Reserve kept interest rates artificially low to help pay for the war. After the fighting stopped in 1918, after a brief period raising interest rates and a fall in wages and stock prices, the Fed decided to lower interest rates in the early 1920s. The Dow Jones rallied along with the cut in interest rates during the 1920s. Stocks were now more attractive than bonds. The stock rally was aided and abetted by the proliferation of buying stock on the margin. Buying stock on the margin occurs when the client borrows money from his stockbroker. By the time the Fed decided to raise interest rates in 1929 to curb the economic bubble, it was too late as it had lost control by that time. Does this sound familiar!? The stock market crashed in October 1929. An excellent book on the Great Depression is A History of the United States in Five Crashes by Scott Nations.

Three events contributed to unemployment in the 1930s—the Smoot-Hawley Tariff, a tax increase, and reduced money supply. The government meant for the Smoot-Hawley Tariff to protect the American worker by increasing the price of foreign products. By raising imported prices, the reasoning goes that domestic products' demand would grow, and thus, American firms would hire more workers. Instead, it diminished consumers' buying power. The increase in taxes further reduced real incomes and consumer demand. When the Federal Reserve increased interest rates by decreasing the money supply, aggregate demand plummeted, aggravating unemployment.

Why did the Fed raise interest rates in the early 1930s? Foreigners were taking their money out of the United States because they feared the unstable American economy. The government considered this money exodus a threat to the economy and figured that if the Fed raised interest rates,

CHAPTER 10: EMPLOYMENT

foreigners would keep their money in the U.S. By 1933, total output in the United States fell one-third from its previous level, and unemployment reached 25 percent. Living conditions worsened as wages collapsed, and there were no unemployment benefits and few social welfare programs. The depression spread to other countries, and suffering intensified, leading the way to massive changes.

MEASURING UNEMPLOYMENT

The U.S. Bureau of Labor Statistics measures employment and unemployment for individuals over the age of 16. The Bureau calculates the unemployment rate by using two different labor force surveys. Full employment exists when four to 6 percent of the workforce is seeking employment. The first method is the Current Population Survey (CPS), also known as the household survey. The Bureau surveys about 60,000 households each month, primarily by knocking on doors. Surveyors make their door-to-door trek, asking questions about the length of job search, age, and status in the household, race, and gender. The Bureau measures the unemployment rate by dividing the number of unemployed persons by the labor force. The second method is the Current Employment Statistics Survey (CES): also known as the payroll survey. The Bureau conducts the CES by sampling 160,000 businesses and government agencies that represent 400,000 individual employees. Discouraged workers are people who would like a job but who have quit looking for work. Discouraged workers can be young people who have postponed looking for a job, students extending their college years, and persons who have applied for long-term disability benefits after losing their jobs. Another category of

CHAPTER 10: EMPLOYMENT

employment is underemployment, which measures the extent of people with jobs below their qualification.

STRUCTURAL UNEMPLOYMENT

Structural unemployment occurs when the skills demanded by employers do not match the talents or location of the unemployed. We know that change is inevitable, and changes in technology sweep out the old and bring in the new, eliminating some jobs and birthing others. For example, DVD rental companies have gone out of business while Netflix has prospered. Blockbuster faced bankruptcy because the owners considered themselves a video rental business, but their business was not rentals. It was entertainment. Microsoft thought that Apple Computer would never succeed with its new and novel device, the iPad. However, Apple sold six million units on the first day while revolutionizing the mobile device industry. All of these events bring about change that alters the economy and job opportunities.

A study from the National Bureau of Economic Research examined the workforce's impact of the workforce between 1990 and 2007. It found that one robot led to the loss of 6.2 jobs within a commuting zone where people travel to work. The study found that robots have contributed to the loss of between 360,000 and 670,000 jobs. This job loss occurred because the economy changed structurally. But does automation necessarily lead to unemployment? Is it a fact that the more robots we have—the fewer jobs? The answer is no. We can have more jobs at the same time that we experience an increase in unemployment. How is this possible? Automation leads to a rise in employment.

CHAPTER 10: EMPLOYMENT

Although, there is a difference between a job opening and someone is filling the position.

Automation generates more jobs because of the lower costs associated with it. A business would not automate if the change did not lower costs. Lower costs lead to lower prices, leading to an increase in consumer demand, which leads to an increase in sales, which leads to an increase in production, which leads to an increase in jobs. There may be unemployment in some localities, but overall, there will be an increase in job opportunities. The kind of jobs lost are the low-skilled jobs, and the jobs generated are high-skilled. So, unemployment is not due to automation; unemployment is due to the failure of the system to find enough educated people to fill the jobs. Education, reasonable regulations, and a simplified tax system are the cures for structural unemployment.

FATCA and STRUCTURAL UNEMPLOYMENT

During the Obama years, the tax evasion tactics of U.S. corporations and wealthy individuals moved Congress to act with the passage of the Foreign Account Tax Compliance Act (FATCA) in 2010 but which took effect in July 2014. FATCA requires that all world financial institutions make available to the U.S. Internal Revenue Service (IRS) complete documentation of their American customers. The IRS will then do due diligence to make sure that people are compliant with American tax laws. If banks fail to report this information, the U.S. government will withhold 30 percent of all monies paid to the financial institution. It is hard to know the long-term impact of this law on foreign relations, but FATCA will set back the American dollar as the world's standard currency.

CHAPTER 10: EMPLOYMENT

The U.S. government will also deny or revoke passports for U.S. citizens who have not paid their taxes. The State Department will block Americans with delinquent tax debt from receiving new visas and will rescind others. Using a threshold of $50,000 of unpaid federal taxes, the Internal Revenue Service compiles a list of affected taxpayers. This provision affects millions of U.S. citizens living abroad who need their passports, including work visas or residency permits, registering a child for school, banking, and checking into a hotel.

Obamacare, the Financial Reform Bill, the impact of the Consumer Financial Protection Bureau, FATCA, tax law changes, and other things have resulted in structural unemployment. U.S. exports have flatlined since the passage of FATCA. Small businesses with less than 500 employees do not have the resources to hire accountants and lawyers, as do large corporations. These structural changes will have an enormous impact on future growth and employment.

STAGFLATION

Historically, economists thought that unemployment and inflation could not coexist. For years, economists believed in the Phillips Curve, which showed an inverse relationship between inflation and unemployment. When we had inflation, we had full employment, and when we had unemployment, we experienced stable or falling prices. In the 1970s, we experienced both problems.

So, can we fight both problems concurrently? The answer depends on whether we consider the short run or the long run. Over the short term, we have few options and must choose which

CHAPTER 10: EMPLOYMENT

of the two is the pressing problem. For example, in the early 1980s, the solution to stagflation occurred when the Fed allowed unemployment to worsen while keeping a tight rein on the money supply to cure the inflation problem. However, by tightening the money supply, authorities caused more unemployment. This policy ushered in one of the worst recessions since the depression of the 1930s in 1981. Once inflation subsided, the Fed eased up on the money supply, and the unemployment problem subsided. In the long run, we have more promising options. We must boost growth by establishing stable monetary policies, reasonable taxes, and regulations despite what we do.

The 1970s was a decade of stagflation due to an increase in costs. Higher labor costs and rising oil prices by the Organization of Petroleum Exporting Countries (OPEC) caused the aggregate supply curve to shift to the left. Labor costs increased because wages increased more than worker's productivity increased.

WHAT TO DO?

Economists agree that increasing productivity is the long-term solution to growing the economy. However, economists disagree on how to use monetary and fiscal policies in the short run. Because Keynesians view the economy as a machine, they favor an activist approach to problems. On the other hand, Austrians support stable policy settings because they adhere to a predetermined set of rules; they tend to ignore short-run fluctuations. For example, the Federal Reserve should increase the money supply each year only to compensate for growth. Austrians believe the government should strive for a balanced budget over the long run, deficits in bad times, and surpluses in

CHAPTER 10: EMPLOYMENT

good times. Whether economists prefer active policies or rules, they agree on three things: we should pay more attention to lag effects, avoid sharp policy changes, and emphasize the long run. Politicians, on the other hand, are moved by politics.

CHAPTER 11:
TRADE & CURRENCY WARS

The world is entering into an era of slowing global trade and an increase in protectionism. We are witnessing something economist John Kenneth Galbraith termed countervailing power where the conflict is between large power blocs, in this case between big business and large foreign customers. Manufacturers have to put down deeper roots in foreign countries to win local business. Conglomerates must agree to buy in the host country. World trade has been dying since the financial crises of 2007 and 2008 as protectionist measures have intensified. Major trading partners such as India, China, Brazil, and Indonesia demand that companies invest and build manufacturing facilities locally and teach local workers new skills and share their technological expertise with the host country.

The Global Trade Alert, a trade monitoring service, counts nearly 350 regulations imposed on companies globally since November of 2008, requiring a larger degree of participation of the host country when bidding for international contracts. As governments have exercised a larger footprint in financial deals, the service has mandated that conglomerates agree to buy or build domestically in exchange for favorable

CHAPTER 11: TRADE & CURRENCY WARS

financing. Baked into the fabric of many international business deals is the requirement that companies must produce thirty to 70 percent of traded products domestically. This trend toward economic nationalization has spread production facilities hurting international trade. As the world becomes less predictable, the US has jumped on board with this new trend by requiring US projects to buy US-made goods. Thus we are witnessing a tug of war between competing demands of national leaders to keep more control at home.

China's Belt and Road Initiative, which envisions reviving ancient trade routes by building Chinese-backed ports, pipelines, and power plants along the road, encompassing 60 percent of world trade, coincides with this new age. The belt refers to an overland transport link across China to Asia and Europe. The road refers to a network of maritime routes connecting China with the middle east, North Africa, and Europe. With the support of the 53 founding member countries, this initiative will transform international trade. The U.S. population is less than 5 percent of the world's population, yet Americans import most of the world's traded goods. Shirts come from Bangladesh, Levi jeans from Mexico, Timberland shoes from Thailand, coffee from Brazil, and bananas from South America. America's top four trading partners are Canada, China, Mexico, and Japan.

In tiny print on the back of an iPhone, Apple assembles the phone in China, but Apple does not manufacture the phone in China. The American Enterprise Institute notes that parts come from South Korea, Japan, Italy, Taiwan, Germany, and the United States. Components of Boeing aircraft wings come from

CHAPTER 11: TRADE & CURRENCY WARS

Japan, South Korea, and Australia. Parts for the fuselages come from Italy, the cargo doors from Sweden, the landing gear doors from Canada, and the engine landing gear from England.

Excessive regulations will starve the U.S. of the resources it needs. American manufacturing has to import 100% of 19 strategic metals. The U.S. has domestic resources for 18 of these 19 metals and minerals, but a maze of government regulations has made mining difficult. Without mining reform, these excessive regulations will starve the U.S. for the resources it needs to build everything from phones to weapons systems. The U.S. is militarily vulnerable because of its dependence on foreigners for many primary metals. Restrictions can cause bottlenecks as these laws cause rigidity in the face of changing market conditions.

The United States and 11 other Pacific Rim nations—Australia, Brunei Darussalam, Canada, Chile, Malaysia, Mexico, New Zealand, Peru, Singapore, Vietnam, and Japan—signed the Trans-Pacific Partnership (TPP) on Feb. 4, 2016. These countries represent 40% of the world's economic output. NAFTA is a 1994 trade agreement between Canada, Mexico, and the United States creating a trilateral trade bloc in North America. Twenty-one percent of America's trade is with these two countries and is the world's largest free trade area.

DOMESTIC VERSUS FOREIGN LABOR

The high wages in America could be less expensive than low wages in other countries on a per-unit basis. Suppose you own a widget business. You have two choices, you can stay in America and pay high salaries, or you can move your business to

CHAPTER 11: TRADE & CURRENCY WARS

Mexico and pay low wages. The increased payments in America could be less expensive, on a per-unit basis, when you consider both inputs and outputs. The money you pay someone is the input and the number of units produced per hour is the output. Suppose you pay the American worker twenty dollars an hour, and he can have two hundred widgets per hour. You pay a Mexican worker a dollar an hour, and he makes only five widgets per hour. On a per-unit basis, the American worker is less expensive despite his higher hourly wage.

In a capital-intensive industry, the benefits of modern infrastructure, an advanced telecommunications network, a highly educated and skilled workforce, and modern technology offset the advantages of low wages. Consequently, high-tech companies in America and low-tech companies, such as textile firms, relocate to places like Bangladesh, where wages are low. Tailors in Bangladesh, who work for global brands, including Tommy Hilfiger, Calvin Klein, and Gap, earn about $40 a month.

ECONOMIES OF SCALE

When a company grows, it experiences larger economies of scale because of a reduction in its long-run average cost curve. For example, a hefty $200,000 tractor is more efficient than a small $25,000 tractor. A farmer who owns 5,000 acres of land can buy the expensive tractor, but the little farmer must use the inefficient tractor. If a country chooses not to trade with other countries, it is like a small, less efficient farmer, and if it does business with other nations, it is like the farmer with 5,000 acres. For example, Boeing Aircraft could not produce its 747 jumbo jets if it could not sell them internationally because the American market is too small to justify the costs.

CHAPTER 11: TRADE & CURRENCY WARS

A country has an absolute advantage if it can produce a good with fewer resources than other countries. Each nation has an absolute advantage in something. For example, Brazil has an absolute advantage in coffee due to its climate and geography. The United States has an absolute advantage in wheat due to its excellent farmland and climate. A country should produce goods whereby it has a comparative advantage. It has a comparative advantage if it can make a product with lower opportunity costs than other nations. A country may have an absolute advantage in a product, but it would be a mistake to produce that product unless it also had a comparative advantage.

BARRIERS TO TRADE

Free and open trade provides the highest efficiencies and living standards for almost everyone; yet, all countries restrict trade through tariffs, quotas, orderly marketing arrangements, and taxes. A tariff is a tax levied on imports. Tariffs bring in revenue, but the government can also impose tariffs to shield American companies from foreign competition. The high tariffs pressure foreign companies to raise their prices to compensate for the tariff, giving American companies a price advantage. Quotas set a maximum quantity that a foreign company can import. When the supply of a good is limited, everything else being equal, the market will dictate a higher price because of the limited quantity. Thus, the quota gives the domestic producer a price advantage over foreign competitors.

CHAPTER 11: TRADE & CURRENCY WARS

WHY RESTRICT TRADE?

If all countries relaxed their trade restrictions, almost all nations would benefit economically. So why do countries restrict trade? Some of the following reasons for trade restrictions are valid, some are not, and some are valid only for some countries at certain times.

- National Defense

A country will not continue a conflict if an enemy restricts the flow of essential war materials. Israel, for example, is a country surrounded by enemies. Even though Israel may not have a comparative advantage in manufacturing guns, it would still produce them. Therefore, trade restrictions that would help protect Israel from its enemies would be justified. There are times when other priorities will take precedence over efficiency.

- Protect Jobs

Protecting domestic jobs from foreign competition is perhaps the weakest justification for trade restrictions because companies can justify almost any protectionist policy. Politicians protect special interest groups because the saved jobs are visible, whereas the jobs lost are not. Tariffs aimed at preserving jobs go against the principle of comparative advantage. A beggar-my-neighbor policy is when countries try to push their employment problems onto other countries, making unemployment like a hot potato. As nations engage in tariff wars, unemployment worsens for everyone. What goes around—comes around.

CHAPTER 11: TRADE & CURRENCY WARS

- Infant Industries

Just as adults need to protect babies, governments need to protect infant industries until they can compete independently. A foreign competitor may have the advantages of established markets and economies of scale, putting the domestic business at a disadvantage. By protecting the domestic market, the company may be able to grow until it can compete successfully. Once the company matures, the government can lift the restrictions. This argument is valid, assuming that politicians are willing to eliminate the protection at some point. The protective policies tend to remain in force because of rent-seeking. When this happens, the economy suffers because the inefficiencies lead to higher prices and fewer choices.

- Dumping

Dumping occurs when foreign governments pay their companies to export, allowing the companies to sell their products to foreigners below cost. Consequently, competing businesses in the importing country ask for protection from their governments. Sometimes these claims are valid, and sometimes they are not. For example, the Commerce Department has dismissed dumping charges lodged against Mexican companies by producers of Florida fruit and vegetables because vegetables are perishable. All growers sell below cost at some point in the season and make it up in others. The US steel industry has demanded protection because of dumping claims. In the past, the US steel industry has argued that trade restrictions were insufficient. Not wanting to offend steel companies, the Commerce Department responded with high tariffs.

CHAPTER 11: TRADE & CURRENCY WARS

Consequently, all businesses that use steel, and all consumers who buy products made from steel, end up paying higher prices. According to the Office of the US Trade Representative, China was the largest source of goods imported to the US, causing a US trade deficit. The US has threatened to take a tougher stance toward China by imposing tariffs and labeling China a currency manipulator. Most US politicians believe that the United States has gotten a raw deal from its major trading partners.

EXCHANGE RATES

When President Nixon closed the gold window in 1971, the world embraced a freely flexible international exchange rate system. Out of desperation, governments gave up trying to control the system and allowed their currencies to float. In other words, nations favored the free market to determine currency values. A dirty float occurs when a country influences the value of its currency.

Some countries peg their currency to a primary currency, usually the U.S. dollar, or a group of currencies. For example, China has a managed float system whereby it pegs the yuan (renminbi) to a basket of major currencies that include the U.S. dollar. A cornerstone of China's economic policy is maintaining the yuan exchange rate to benefit its exports. China's central bank has used its foreign reserves to support the yuan. How China manages its currency is one of the most consequential decisions in global financial markets.

Argentina has pegged its currency, the Argentine peso, to the U.S. dollar. When the dollar increased in value, so did the

CHAPTER 11: TRADE & CURRENCY WARS

peso, enabling consumers to buy less expensive foreign products while neglecting to buy the more expensive domestic products, forcing Argentina businesses into bankruptcy.

More than 60% of all foreign currency reserves in the world are in U.S. dollars. In a freely flexible international exchange rate system, interest rates, the expected inflation rate, and the stability of a country influence demand for a currency. People want to keep their money to earn a decent return, where the inflation rate is low and where the money would be safe. In the past, the American dollar met all these needs. Although the American dollar remains stable, only the future will tell what effect changing world events will have on its value. The demand for the American dollar remained strong because the Petrodollar System made the dollar the world's standard currency. Even though the euro is the second largest traded currency next to the American dollar, a European company still has to convert euros to dollars for international transactions.

Today, more than 60% of all foreign currency reserves in the world are in U.S. dollars—but there are changes on the horizon as some countries are making mutual agreements. China and Russia have been quietly arranging to move away from the U.S. dollar over the past few years. China and Japan struck a deal, which will promote their currencies when trading with each other. China and the United Arab Emirates have agreed to ditch the U.S. dollar and use their currencies in oil transactions. When nations demand fewer dollars, the value of the dollar on the world market declines. The UN Conference on Trade and Development (UNCTAD) has declared that the current system is not working, and countries should replace the system with a new managed float system.

CHAPTER 11: TRADE & CURRENCY WARS

The standard of living for the average American will fall when the dollar is no longer the world's standard currency because buying power will decline. When another currency, or a group of currencies, or a cryptocurrency, replaces the dollar, the demand for the dollar will subside, and the dollar's value will diminish. The decline in the dollar's value will also make it more difficult for America to pay interest on its national debt because each dollar given to foreigners will have a lower value.

CURRENCY WARS

A country can achieve a competitive advantage when its currency falls in value relative to other currencies because its products become less expensive to foreigners. A low-valued currency hurts consumers and debtors but favors long-term growth with an increase in foreign demand. At the same time, foreign goods become more expensive, so less money leaves the country. Therefore, nations may compete in a currency war by lowering the value of their currencies. Currency wars are always a zero-sum game. Countries engage in currency wars by influencing the demand and supply of their currency on the world market. Currency wars are always a zero-sum game where someone wins, and someone loses. Countries with high valued currencies are like people who spend all their money without saving; they sacrifice the future for present consumption. Countries with low valued currencies sacrifice current consumption for future gain.

Switzerland has pegged its currency, the franc, to the euro. When market pressures tended to increase the franc relative's value relative to the euro, Swiss banking authorities increased the supply of francs to bring the value down, keeping it

CHAPTER 11: TRADE & CURRENCY WARS

at par with the euro. When their efforts proved ineffective, the Swiss lifted the peg and let the franc seek market equilibrium. The franc's value shot up almost overnight, to where it would have been without the peg. Instead of changes taking place slowly over several years, giving everyone a chance to adjust to the changing conditions, panic and disruptions occurred.

America is in a unique position when it comes to a currency war with other nations. The Federal Reserve's practice of quantitative easing has led to an increase in dollars abroad and has put downward pressure on its value. At the same time, the demand for the dollar remains high because of its status. Another reason the dollar can stay strong in the early stages of a currency war is that value is relative. If other currencies depreciate, then the American dollar may fall in absolute terms but rises in relative terms. Fed officials are not as concerned with a revaluation of the American dollar because America is less dependent on foreign trade than other nations. Exports account for only 13% of U.S. economic output. Even though a stronger dollar weighs on exports, the broader economic impact is limited. Moreover, a stronger dollar means that Americans will pay less for imported oil, which can boost the economy.

No global economic system can prosper if countries only look out for themselves. The strong dollar can hurt multinational corporations in several ways. A high valued dollar can harm U.S. companies that have a presence in foreign countries. Companies' sales may increase in the international market, but when they convert foreign currency back into American dollars, the real return on investment takes a big hit. The changing currency values can also cause a mismatch between costs and sales. This mismatch makes it more difficult for export-oriented companies to compete. To make matters worse, the adverse effects of a

CHAPTER 11: TRADE & CURRENCY WARS

currency revaluation can damage the value of a corporation's stock price.

When the world's central banks abandon their responsibility for global exchange-rate movements, the whole world shakes. When each national bank pursues its monetary policy for domestic purposes, it becomes a race to the bottom in this interconnected world of fiat currencies. No global economic system can prosper if countries only look out for themselves without regard to how their actions affect other countries. Currency wars hurt everyone. Should countries abandon fiscal and monetary restraint and impose trade restrictions on other nations, the world will slip into a depression.

ADJUSTMENTS

A favorable balance of trade, or a trade surplus, occurs when more money enters the country than leaves via trade. However, there are other ways money can enter or leave a country. For example, when Americans travel abroad, money leaves, and when foreigners visit America, money enters. The term balance of payments refers to money entering or leaving a country. With a net inflow of money, we have a favorable balance of payments, sometimes called a payments surplus. With a net outflow of funds, we have an unfavorable balance of payments, sometimes called a payments deficit.

A freely flexible international exchange-rate system will automatically correct a country's balance of payments problem. For example, suppose that the United States has a deficit problem with too much money leaving the country. As dollars become more abundant on the international market, their value will

CHAPTER 11: TRADE & CURRENCY WARS

decrease, making foreign goods more expensive for Americans and American goods cheaper for foreigners. A reversal occurs when Americans buy less from foreigners, and foreigners buy more from Americans.

What happens if America experiences a payments surplus? With more dollars entering the country than leaving, the supply of dollars on the global market decreases, making the dollar worth more. Now Americans will buy more from foreigners, and foreigners will purchase less from America. This reversal eliminates the problem of too much money entering the country. Thus, over time, the economy tends to point where the amount of money leaving equals the money entering a country.

INTERNATIONAL MONETARY FUND

Countries with a balance of payments problem can borrow money from the International Monetary Fund (IMF) through Special Drawing Rights (SDR's), composed of mixed currencies. Suppose the value of the dollar were to plummet. The U.S. government could then approach other countries, such as Germany and Japan, and request that the IMF transfer United States SDRs to their accounts. In return, Germany and Japan would supply the United States with euros and yen. The United States could then use the euros and yen to buy dollars worldwide, thus increasing the dollar's value.

The Chinese yuan has been included as the fifth currency in the International Monetary Fund as a Special Drawing Right (SDR). This inclusion reflects the ongoing evolution of the global economy and is a significant change for the IMF. The yuan's addition is the first since the fund adopted the euro as a part of

CHAPTER 11: TRADE & CURRENCY WARS

the basket of funds. The inclusion acknowledges the advances China has made in improving the infrastructure of its financial markets.

A flexible international exchange-rate system with selective intervention, a managed float system can solve some currency problems quickly, but only stable economies will stabilize currencies over the long run. Despite what a nation does to influence its exchange rate, instability will cause foreigners to flee that country's currency over the long run.

THE EXPORT-IMPORT BANK

The Export-Import Bank helps U.S. companies sell products to foreign customers, mainly by providing or guaranteeing loans when private banks will not. The top beneficiaries have been big businesses. Many other countries have similar banks, including China, Japan, South Korea, and most European countries. Some economists believe the bank is a prime example of crony capitalism and distorts the free market to benefit a few connected corporations. Think rent-seeking—those who pay can play. The bank also poses a risk to taxpayers.

NEOCONSERVATIVES

Countries often make trade decisions for non-economic reasons influenced by the Neoconservatives of the deep state regardless of who occupies the White House. The Neoconservatives are motivated more by power and control and less by profit. Once countries try to break away from the clutches of the Neoconservatives, they know they might face military action. Egypt, Saudi, Arabia, Iraq, Syria, Sudan, Venezuela, and

CHAPTER 11: TRADE & CURRENCY WARS

other countries are looking to purchase the Russian-made S-400 anti-aircraft surface-to-air missile defense system to protect their country from the deep state. Turkey has finalized a $2.5 billion deal to buy the S-400. The S-400 has been considered one of the most effective surface-to-air missile systems in the world. Saudi's agreement with Russia could indicate a political shift by Saudi Arabia to turn away from its historically the United States. A nail was put into the coffin of the PetroDollar System when Russia signed a memorandum of understanding to help Saudi Arabia in its efforts to develop its military industries. These countries are mindful of Libyan leader Muammar al-Gaddafi, who planned to create a gold-backed African currency to compete with the dollar and euro.

CHAPTER 12:
DEPRESSIONS

Conditions during the Great Depression were fertile ground for the ideas of John M. Keynes and demand management economics; the Depression paved the way for a broader role of the federal government and the Federal Reserve. After the Employment Act of 1946 empowered the federal government to pursue maximum employment. After Congress cemented this commitment with the Humphrey-Hawkins Act in 1978, which mandated the Fed to seek full employment and stable prices, the government fully embraced the ideas of Keynesian economics. Keynesians believe that with proper econometric models, the government can make wise decisions and moderate the business cycle swings with monetary and fiscal policies.

Keynesians believe the Humphrey-Hawkins Act strengthened the Full Employment Act of 1946, while Austrians postulate it weakened the government's role by imposing impossible mandates on the Federal Reserve. The Fed will increase the money supply during periods of unemployment and reduce the money supply during inflationary times, but it cannot do both with stagflation. Austrians criticize these mandates because they are more reactive rather than proactive. Instead of

CHAPTER 12: DEPRESSIONS

concentrating on long-run growth, it forces authorities to stress the short run.

FANNIE MAE & FREDDIE MAC

Fan and Fred do not make loans; they buy loans. Congress established Fannie Mae in 1938 and Freddie Mac in 1970 with a federal line of credit to moderate the business cycle and add liquidity to the mortgage market. Banks do not keep mortgages; they sell them to Fan and Fred. The bank can now make another mortgage loan, sell it, make another, and so forth. Congress figured that this would juice the mortgage market and lead to more growth and opportunities for everyone. Fan and Fred profit from this arrangement by securitizing the loans.

Securitization is the process of repackaging loans into a financial asset and dividing the asset into three different tiers (called tranches), and then selling off bits and pieces to investors. The best are in the top, and high-risk loans are in the bottom layer, the toxic waste category. Economists call this collection of loans a Collateralized Debt Obligation (CDO) or a Mortgage-Backed Security (MBS) if the loans are mortgages. Since banks sell their loans to Fan and Fred, they are less concerned about the creditworthiness of their clients.

THE FED TOOK ACTION in 2008

Economists call these securitized loans a Collateralized Debt Obligation (CDO). In 2008, the rapidly eroding confidence in the financial system caused several major financial firms to collapse. Banks and insurance companies faced bankruptcy, and private citizens experienced enormous losses. Fearing that

CHAPTER 12: DEPRESSIONS

conditions could cause a depression, the Federal Reserve took action to stem the tide by doing business with Fan, Fred, and commercial banks. First, it agreed to purchase debt instruments from Fan and Fred, and then it committed itself to exchange billions of dollars of risk-free federal bonds for high-risk private bonds held by commercial entities. These actions helped relieve the panic, and conditions improved. Just as JP Morgan and others envisioned in 1913, the Federal Reserve saved the day by being a lender of last resort.

TOO BIG TO FAIL?

Keynesians support bailouts because they believe that the failure of large corporations will systematically lead to a full-fledged economic collapse. Austrians argue that the practice prevents the economy from finding its floor and thus inhibits the system from seeking equilibrium. For example, General Motors (GM) was losing billions of dollars per year by 2009. For years, GM routinely agreed to generous labor contracts with the United Auto Workers Union (UAW). By the 2007-2008 recession hit, GM was uncompetitive due to high labor and pension costs. Previously, the company would have declared bankruptcy, and the bankruptcy courts would have sorted out who gets what. Other businesses would have purchased the assets of GM and started producing cars. Instead, the government, with help from the Canadian government, granted loans to GM. This arrangement allowed GM to continue business with all its baggage intact. International authorities have bailed out whole nations. For example, the World Bank granted Greece a series of loan extensions for years. Puerto Rico, a U.S. territory, has defaulted on billions of dollars of loans and declared bankruptcy

CHAPTER 12: DEPRESSIONS

in May 2017. When these international events occur, the solutions are tricky because international bankruptcy laws are non-existent. Loan defaults hurt both the debtors and creditors and can quickly spread, making bailouts impossible.

RULES vs PRINCIPLES

Austrians support principles, and Keynesians favor rules. Rules affect every aspect of our lives. Businesses have to perform numerous studies before they can build anything. The No Child Left Behind Law dictates what students learn in each grade, forcing teachers to teach to the test. Strict rules throw spontaneity and creativity out the window. Everyone has to know the rules, and everyone has to comply. COVID-19 has accentuated this trend.

Everyone has to know the rules, and everyone has to comply with the rules. When a doctor sees a Medicare or Medicaid patient, a specialist must verify that the patient falls under one of the 140,000 different categories for the physician to receive payment. In this world of rules, no human being is in charge—we are all subject to the letter of the law—and once authorities establish the rules, they are almost impossible to change. Each government agency has guidelines. Government guidelines are a way of establishing standards without the legality of mandatory regulations. Businesses are troubled when the Labor Department has one set of rules, and the IRS has a different set of rules. For example, there is a one hundred-page FDA rule requiring calorie counts of pizza toppings!

Principles provide broad goals while leaving human beings in charge. For example, nursing homes should be safe and

CHAPTER 12: DEPRESSIONS

clean and should serve wholesome food; someone is in charge when principles apply. Some local person has the authority to make sure the nursing home meets the spirit of the law. There is always someone who can enforce the principles. An economy based on principles, on the other hand, is flexible and better equipped to adapt to changing conditions. Philip K. Howard writes about rules in his book *The Rule of Nobody – Saving America from Dead Laws and Broken Government*. Howard explains how the rules constrain and bog down nations. In a world of rules, no one is in charge because the rules rule instead of people. Rules have replaced principles, and everyone is affected.

John Yates is the captain of Miss Katie. He was fishing for grouper in the Gulf of Mexico when the Florida Fish and Wildlife Commissioner boarded his boat for a routine inspection. The Commissioner charged Mr. Yates with having aboard 72 grouper fish smaller than the 20 inches allowed. When he got into port, federal officials counted only 69 undersized fish. The agents charged him with violating the anti-shredding provision of the Sarbanes-Oxley Act, which carries a 20-year prison term. John Yates was a victim of the ruling when no one with common sense was in charge.

The Justice Department has used rules to extract multi-million-dollar settlements from banks. For example, the Department has applied fines to lenders for not having a quality-control process that follows Federal Housing Administration guidelines. If there are mistakes, such as misstating a borrower's income by a tiny amount, the Justice Department can hold lenders liable for up to three times damages.

CHAPTER 12: DEPRESSIONS

Howard's explanation of rules is similar to the ideas of the Austrian economist Friedrich Hayek. In *The Road to Serfdom*, Hayek explains how excessive planning leads to losing all personal freedom. When planners realize that the only way to work is to mandate that everyone adhere to the program, the road serfdom is complete. Some countries are moving away from a rule-based system. Australia moved toward a principles-based system when it replaced all its rules for nursing homes with 31 principles; for example, nursing homes must have a homelike setting, and there should be space for privacy, etc. Instead of making structural changes, we have thrown money at our problems and passed laws that have bound our financial system in a web of rules and regulations. If we are going to repair our economic system, we must understand the causes of the largest meltdown in history.

THE FINANCIAL CRISES OF 2007-2008

The financial crisis of 2007-2008 is a story of intrigue, secret dealings, ambition, greed, and epic battles where heroes are villains and villains are heroes. So how is it that the world's financial system stood on the brink of total collapse? How is it that a domino effect of loan defaults came perilously close to throwing the world into economic darkness? What are the events that led to the financial crisis of 2007-2008? Can it happen again?

We begin our story with the Community Reinvestment Act (CRA) of 1977, which Congress amended in 1989, 1995, and 2005. This Act promoted banking services to all members of a community and prohibited redlining, which is refusing a loan to someone because they live in a poor neighborhood. Banks make

CHAPTER 12: DEPRESSIONS

prime loans to creditworthy customers and make subprime loans to people with poor credit scores. The Community Reinvestment Act popularized subprime loans with relaxed lending standards. Thus, low or no money down, variable or adjustable rate, Alt-A, and negative amortization loans became popular.

The subprime loans in the early 2000s caused a housing bubble. Adjustable-rate mortgages begin with low-interest rates, called teaser rates, and increase yearly according to a fixed schedule. Alt-A loans (nicknamed liar loans) are loans whereby bank officials do not ask borrowers to verify credit information on their applications. Negative amortization loans are loans whereby the mortgagee borrows money with every monthly payment—the payment does not cover all the interest owed—so after five years or so, debtors owe more than when they started. By the end of the decade, almost 40% of all U.S. mortgages, 25 million loans, were low-quality loans. The proliferation of subprime loans and the low interest rates in the early 2000s caused a housing bubble.

Besides putting pressure on banks to meet the needs of low-income people, in 1992, Congress gave a new affordable housing mission to Fannie Mae and Freddie Mac and authorized the Department of Housing and Urban Development to impose lower underwriting standards for the twins. Before this, Fan and Fred bought prime mortgages, but now Congress required them to meet quotas for subprime loans. Eventually, Fan and Fred would buy more than $1 trillion of subprime loans from banks, representing about 40 percent of all mortgages.

In 1993, President Clinton teamed up with Roberta Achtenberg, the assistant secretary of the Department of Housing and Urban Development (HUD), to increase homeownership in

CHAPTER 12: DEPRESSIONS

poor and minority communities. Roberta began to threaten, harass, and bully banks into providing mortgages to people who previously did not qualify for loans. As a result, between 1993 and 1999, more than two million low-income people became new homeowners. She set up a national grid of offices staffed by attorneys and investigators who enforced anti-discrimination laws against banks. Finally, banks acquiesced and started to make thousands of lenient loans and, in some cases, without requiring a down payment. A healthy mortgage market in the mid to late 1990s made mortgage defaults minimal, but these unhealthy loans sowed the seeds of an economic meltdown.

Politicians have spent years arguing that private lenders created the housing bubble and that Fan and Fred went along for the ride. The Securities and Exchange Commission begs to differ. The SEC issued a report showing how Fran and Fred turbocharged the crisis by degrading their underwriting standards to increase their subprime loans to satisfy the Community Reinvestment Act requirements. Under pressure to meet government mandates, Fan and Fred needed help. Help came in 1999 when they teamed up with Countrywide Home Loans Company, a company specializing in a reduced documentation loan program called the Fast and Easy Loan. Angelo Mozilo, Countrywide's founder, and Fannie were business partners in the subprime mortgage market. Countrywide found the customers while Fan purchased the mortgages from Countrywide. As Fan expanded its subprime loan purchases and guarantees, the SEC alleges that executives hid the risk level from investors.

President Bush pushed hard to expand home ownership, especially among minority groups. In October of 2002, President Bush stated, *"We can put light where there's darkness, and hope where there's despondency in this country. And part of it is*

CHAPTER 12: DEPRESSIONS

working together as a nation to encourage folks to own their home." Bush pushed hard to expand home ownership, especially among minority groups. On December 16, 2003, he signed the American Dream Down Payment Act. This act doubled the funds for housing counseling services, made it easier for potential buyers to shop around and compare prices and simplified forms. This encouraged more people to apply for a mortgage loan.

Throughout the 2000s, Fan and Fred increased their purchases of subprime mortgage loans. These policies did not initially cause problems, but they began adding fuel to the fire in 2007. When millions of homeowners defaulted on their mortgages in 2007 and 2008, Fan and Fred lost billions. Thus, they relinquished their quasi-government status and reverted to complete government control in 2008. Presently, Fan and Fred own most mortgages in America. With only a 3 percent down payment, a modest decline in home prices puts new home buyers underwater, meaning they owed more on their house than what the house was worth. Deflation in home prices trapped homeowners when they needed to relocate or could no longer make their mortgage payments. A lack of equity forced them to sell at a loss or default.

EXCESSIVE LEVERAGE

Because the government forced banks to invest in risky loans, banks were eager to increase their profits in the derivatives market. According to one of the world's leading derivatives experts, Paul Wilmott, who holds a doctorate in applied mathematics from Oxford University, the notional value of the derivatives market is more than a quadrillion dollars, making it more than five times the world's GDP. The unregulated

CHAPTER 12: DEPRESSIONS

derivatives market contributed to the crash of 2008. If participants in the derivatives market use their own money, there may not be a problem. However, this was not the case in 2008, and it is not the case today.

Suppose you have authority over a large sum of money, such as a retirement fund or a country's finances, such as Iceland. One day, a Bear Stearns Investment Bank (Bear is now a part of JP Morgan Chase Bank) walks into your office and asks if you are interested in buying security. The security, a bond, has a triple-A rating and has a history of paying a 25% return. *"Wow that's a great deal—what is it?"* So he says, *"Hey, I'm busy—do you want this or not"* Bear Stearns has an excellent reputation, and the security has the highest credit rating, so you take the deal without knowing the particulars. Unfortunately, few people knew what they were buying in the derivatives market, leading to the financial collapse because this was an over-the-counter market, an unregulated market.

The crisis became a financial meltdown of epic proportions. When the government established the Securities and Exchange Commission (SEC) in 1934, it set banks' debt to capital ratio at 12 to one. A ratio of 12 to one means that a bank had to have at least one dollar in reserve to lend out 12 dollars. However, the SEC abolished this debt-to-net-capital rule in 2004 when it allowed large investment banks to determine their debt to income levels based on their risk management computer models. So instead of adhering to the twelve-to-one ratio, the new norm became forty-to-one; banks could invest 40 dollars with only one dollar in reserve.

The forty to one debt to capital ratio made enormous profits possible in the derivatives market. But, when the economy

CHAPTER 12: DEPRESSIONS

began to head south in 2007, this excessive leverage led to the collapse of all five investment banks, Goldman Sachs, Bear Stearns, Morgan Stanley, Merrill Lynch, and Lehman Brothers. Lehman had assets worth $691 billion. In comparison, when GM went bankrupt several years later, it had assets worth just $91 billion. By September 2008, the crisis had become a crisis of epic proportions. To stem the tide, the Federal Reserve allowed these investment banks to purchase commercial banks, and thus the Fed granted these new entities holding bank status. A bank holding company is a large corporation that owns a bank. The Fed offers holding companies the same protection that it provides to commercial banks.

BROOKSLEY BORN

There is no way of knowing the facts with an over-the-counter market except what the seller wishes to divulge. One of the few persons who saw a danger in the derivatives market was Brooksley Born, the Commodity Futures Trading Commission (CFTC.). The CFTC is the federal agency that oversees the futures and commodity options markets. Brooksley was the chairperson of the CFTC from August 1996 to June 1999.

The government authorized the CFTC to detect fraud in the over-the-counter derivatives market without an exchange. There is no way of knowing the facts with an over-the-counter market except what the seller wishes to divulge. When she looked into the market, she became concerned about the dangers it posed to the entire economy. As chair of the CFTC, she was aware of how quickly the over-the-counter derivatives market was growing and how little federal regulators knew about it. Brooksley saw fraud and over-speculation leading to dramatic

CHAPTER 12: DEPRESSIONS

failures. One example is Orange County, California, which went bankrupt because of high-risk bets in the derivatives market. In Iceland, three of the country's central privately owned commercial banks failed. Iceland's systemic banking collapse was the most significant experienced by any country in history.

Iceland is an example of one of the most remarkable recoveries in history and is a testament to the resiliency of sound fiscal policies. Within three years, Iceland rose from the ashes while experiencing a robust economy. Because banks are high-tech corporations, when they collapsed, there was a plethora of technology talent on the market, which companies could reasonably hire. In addition, because the technology sector is more creative than the banking sector, Iceland could grow again.

Iceland has implemented policies contrary to Western practices, including the United States. Iceland was more concerned about its democracy than it was about its financial markets. Once a country sacrifices the democratic elements of its society for economic expediency, it begins to slide down the slippery slope toward tyranny. Contrary to the prevailing orthodoxy, instead of bailing out the bankers, Iceland imprisoned many of them, and insolvent banks were allowed to fail. Instead of creating money to bail out the financial system, Iceland supported its citizens according to a public referendum. The IMF and the World Bank were highly critical of the country; China was the only country that helped Iceland.

Brooksley Born was more like Olafur Ragnar Grimsson, the President of Iceland during and after the collapse than she was to the American leadership. Brooksley was concerned because few in government even knew about derivatives, yet all the big banks were dealers in the market. Her concern was that a

CHAPTER 12: DEPRESSIONS

major default in the market could cause a domino effect throughout the economy. For example, Proctor & Gamble lost $200 billion and sued its derivative dealer, Bankers Trust, for fraud, alleging that the bank had sold them complex derivatives without proper explanation. Finally, in 1996, Bankers Trust settled with Proctor & Gamble, forgiving most of the debt.

Now here is where things get interesting. When Brooksley contacted the Treasury Department, the Federal Reserve, and the Securities and Exchange Commission about her concerns, not only were they complacent, but they questioned whether Brooksley had the authority to take action. So why was Alan Greenspan, who was Chairman of the Federal Reserve from 1987 to 2006, opposed to any oversight of the derivatives market? Alan Greenspan is a disciple of Ayn Rand, who wrote the book, *Atlas Shrugged* in 1957. Rand believed that the market should be free of all government regulations. So, here we have the Chairman of the Federal Reserve, who handles regulating the banking system, opposed to regulation. Yet, when Brooksley had a private conversation with Alan Greenspan and pointed out extensive fraud in the derivatives market, he responded that the CFTC should not persecute fraud because it would take care of it.

Events took a turn when banks rescued Long-term Capital, a hedge fund, from bankruptcy in 1998 when it was on the losing side of a derivative contract. The banks told Congress that the LTCM problem was the exception to the rule and was not indicative of the derivatives market. Congress accepted this argument and passed the Commodity Futures Modernization Act (CFMA) of 2000. The CFMA stripped the Commodity Futures Trading Commission of all responsibility for derivatives and forbade the Securities and Exchange Commission (SEC) and state regulators from interfering with the market.

CHAPTER 12: DEPRESSIONS

CREDIT DEFAULT SWAPS (CDSs)

In addition to the Community Reinvestment Act, the subprime mortgage market, and the expanding derivatives market, credit default swaps, and collateralized debt obligations played a role in the economic crisis of 2007-2008. The whiz kids of JP Morgan Bank met in Boca Raton, Florida, in the early 1990s and barnstormed ways to convince the Fed to reduce the bank's reserve requirement. Thus, the credit default swap (CDS) was born. A credit default swap occurs when one party pays another party to assume the risk of default. It is like a written insurance policy, a legal agreement, against loan losses whereby the purchaser of the swap transfers defaults risk to the seller. In the event of a default, the seller makes payment to the buyer of the swap. Credit default swaps convinced the Fed that banks' loss exposure had diminished and agreed to lower the bank's reserve requirement. Thus, the CDS succeeded in its original intent. Unfortunately, the bad news came later when buyers and the sellers of swaps abused this sound business practice. A closer look at these swaps and how they were instrumental in exasperating the financial collapse of 2007-2008 will enlighten your understanding of the economic collapse.

CREDIT DEFAULT SWAPS AND REAL INSURANCE

The buyer of a CDS pays the seller quarterly, semiannually, or annually. Credit-default swaps have value because investors can buy and sell them. Whoever owns the CDS receives payments from the purchaser, just as an insurance company receives payments from customers. Economists consider a CDS a derivative because the underlying bonds determine its value.

CHAPTER 12: DEPRESSIONS

Actual insurance policies guard against irresponsibility and fraud. Unlike CDSs, insurance policies have provisions for deductibles, policy limits, and higher premiums for high risks. You cannot buy an insurance policy on your house twenty times its value, especially if it has burned down five times in the last decade. You cannot purchase home insurance if you do not own a home. If you have five convictions for drunk driving, you may not be able to buy automobile insurance, and if you can, it will be costly—not so with credit default swaps.

Unlike real insurance, credit default swaps have no deductibles or policy limits and place no constraints on buyers. If you have the money, there is no limit to the quantity, even on the securities, you do not own. A naked credit default swap means you take out insurance on bonds without actually owning them. You can bet that either the security or the company issuing the security will fail. Wall Street was able to sell high-risk securities because sellers convinced buyers that CDSs could protect them from loss. With CDSs, as long as someone was willing to sell them, there was no limit to the liabilities.

CREDIT DEFAULT SWAPS and CDOs

Credit default swaps and collateralized debt obligations are sound business practices. The problem was not the practice but in the types of loans that banks securitized in combination with sales volume. If the securitized loans had met at least minimum standards of creditworthiness, they would not have been a problem. However, financial firms securitized high-risk loans in the toxic waste category. When the bankers of JP Morgan, the originator of the credit default swap, learned that

CHAPTER 12: DEPRESSIONS

other banks were forming swaps made up of junk bonds, they were appalled.

Despite the dealings in high-risk loans, securitization would not have been a problem if the transactions were small, which they were not. The book, *Two Trillion Dollar Meltdown – Easy Money, High Rollers, and the Great Credit Crash* of explaining how we got into a credit crunch, Charles Morris does an excellent job in his book *Two Trillion Dollar Meltdown*. He explores the financial markets, the policy misjudgments, and the delusions that led to a giant credit bubble in history. In addition, he explains how excessive debt led to a massive disruption in global markets and how government leaders are still downplaying the problem.

CDOs, CDSs & CREDIT RATINGS

Government and retirement funds mandate that their investments must be of the highest credit rating, Triple-A. Standard and Poor's and Moody's are credit rating agencies that corporations pay to assess their debt instruments. So how is it that these agencies gave CDOs made up of junk bonds a triple-A rating? Now Joe Cassano, head of the Financial Products Division of American International Group (AIG) from 2001 to 2008, enters the picture. AIG is an insurance and financial services conglomerate that was once the largest insurer in the world. The Financial Products Division and Joe Cassano made billions of dollars for AIG.

Because the government did not regulate the CDS market, Cassano could sell as many credit default swaps as he wanted without considering how the company would pay the claims in

CHAPTER 12: DEPRESSIONS

the event of massive defaults. However, unbeknownst to buyers, the finances of the Financial Products Division and its parent company, AIG, could not be co-mingled. Investors had a misconception of the relationship between the parent company, AIG, and its subsidiary, the Financial Products Division. The Financial Products Division was self-financed; the parent company's finances were not available to the Financial Products Division. As a result, investors assumed that they were the same entities. Consequently, Cassano was able to sell credit default swaps without sufficient collateral to back them.

Banks argued that when they purchased a credit default swap from AIG on a collateralized debt obligation, the CDO should have a triple-A rating because AIG had a triple-A rating. Therefore, even though there was a likelihood of default, the risk level was low because AIG backed the CDO. In other words, investors in the CDO were safe because AIG would pay if people stopped making their payments, or so they thought. When the government accepted this argument, Cassano was able to sell billions of dollars worth of credit default swaps without enough collateral. Banks could now sell billions of dollars value of junk CDOs because of their triple-A rating. able to sell credit default swaps without sufficient collateral to back them.

The SEC did not regulate the industry, so Cassano operated with no restraints, and investors were not privy to all the facts. As a result, when the bubble burst in 2007, AIG was on the hook for billions of dollars while lacking sufficient funds to make good on its credit default swaps. Thus, AIG needed a government bailout. An excellent book on the subject is Fool's Gold by Gillian Tett. The book explains how the economic collapse of 2007 and 2008 was self-inflicted. Ms. Tett explains how financial incentives within banks and other financial firms and the rating

CHAPTER 12: DEPRESSIONS

agencies warped regulatory structures. The book is a fascinating read because she explores the human foibles that led to the collapse.

THE COLLAPSE!

The easy money policies of the Federal Reserve during the 1990s, the deregulation mania, and excessive leverage resulted in the bubble bursting. Now add some greed to the mix, throw in some hubris, add stupidity, and we have all the ingredients of a massive collapse! When the housing market collapsed in 2007-2008, many homeowners found themselves upside down on their mortgage; they owed more on their house than its value. What made matters worse is that homeowners took out equity loans, using their appreciated houses as collateral. The bubble burst when people stopped making their mortgage payments.

Marking to market accounting played a role in the ensuing downturn. Marking to market is the practice of revaluing an asset according to the price it would fetch on the open market, regardless of what the owner paid for it. Once the market headed south, investors who had bought assets on the margin were subject to margin calls as the value of their assets dwindled. Problems occur when banks abuse sound business practices. When you buy an asset on the margin, you borrow money from your stockbroker or your lender. You experience a margin call when the lender demands payment of the loan. Sometimes this is referred to as a "call market." The margin calls forced many investors into bankruptcy.

CHAPTER 12: DEPRESSIONS

What has Congress done about the problem? Rather than penalizing the abusers, Congress has criminalized honest mistakes, poor judgment, and ignorance. It has created an atmosphere of fear and intimidation, increasing mergers of big corporations and a decline in the small business market.

THE STUDENT LOAN MARKET

So what is the current situation with securitizing debt into CDOs? Securitization is alive and well in the student loan market. Asset-Backed Securities (ABS) financed a significant portion of the student loan boom. Students owe more than $1 trillion to the federal government; this debt exceeds total credit card debt. At the peak of the housing market collapse in 2007-2008, 10 percent of homeowners fell behind on their payments. The Federal Reserve Bank of New York has found that 44% of student borrowers are not making payments. According to the Department of Education, students borrow more than $100 billion annually, which rises each year.

INSIDE JOB

Inside Job is a documentary film narrated by Matt Damon, which provides a comprehensive analysis of the global financial crisis of 2007-2008. Through exhaustive research and extensive interviews, the film traces the rise of a financial sector that went rogue and had an enormous impact on politics and academia. This film is very entertaining and full of information. In my opinion, this is the best documentary film you will find that captures the essence of the financial crisis that almost destroyed the economy of the nation and the world.

CHAPTER 12: DEPRESSIONS

GRACE and SIMPSON-BOWLES

President Reagan established the Grace Commission in 1984. For two years, 160 corporate executives and community leaders led an army of 2,000 volunteers to root out government waste. Volunteer contributors with zero cost to the federal government funded the search. As a result, the Grace Commission made 2,478 recommendations to cut costs without eliminating essential services. The Grace Commission is a document that covers 21,000 pages laying out a detailed plan to make the federal government more efficient and accountable to the American taxpayer.

Congress passed the Gramm-Rudman-Hollings Act in 1985 as a follow-up to the Grace Commission, otherwise known as the Balanced Budget and Emergency Deficit Control Act. This act made it mandatory for the government to live within its income. The law provided automatic spending cuts to take effect if the president and Congress failed to reach established spending targets. The act gave the U.S. comptroller general authority to order spending cuts when necessary to meet the stated goals. The courts declared the law unconstitutional, and Congress passed a revised version of the bill in 1987.

Instead of implementing needed reform and adhering to the law, Congress found ways to increase borrowing and spending. President Obama formed the Simpson-Bowles Commission, co-chaired by Erskine Bowles and Alan Simpson, to find remedies for the credit crisis in 2010. The Commission outlined an ambitious package of spending cuts and tax increases. The plan called for deep cuts in spending, a gradual rise in the federal gasoline tax, limiting popular tax breaks, the child tax credit, and the earned-income tax credit. It also called for an

CHAPTER 12: DEPRESSIONS

increase in the retirement age for Social Security and gave options for overhauling the tax system. It called for cutting Pentagon weapons programs and reducing cost-of-living increases for all federal programs, including Social Security. Following is an excerpt from the document's preamble. *"We cannot play games or put off hard choices. Without regard to party, we have a patriotic duty to keep the promise of America to give our children and grandchildren a better life."*

Our challenge is clear and inescapable: America cannot be great if we are broke. Our businesses will not be able to grow and create jobs, and our workers will not be able to compete successfully for jobs of the future without a plan to get this crushing debt burden off our backs. The Simpson-Bowles Commission recognizes that the ultimate solution to our economic problems is growth. Real, sustainable growth can only happen when society uses sufficient savings and provides incentives for productive investments. There is no easy fix to our problems, and no amount of creditism will grow the economy in the long run. Although more than 60% of Congress supported its recommendations, the report did not see the light of day. Politicians have chosen to ignore the findings and recommendations of the Simpson-Bowles Commission.

Many nations and municipalities are paying the price of prolific spending and borrowing while ignoring pro-growth policies. The longer the United States refuses to heed the warnings of the Grace Commission, the Simpson-Bowles Commission, and the Gramm-Rudman-Hollings Act, the more massive the subsequent collapse. Then there is the increase in military spending and significant increases in infrastructure spending. Can we grow the economy enough not to have to increase the multi-trillion dollars of the national debt?

CHAPTER 12: DEPRESSIONS

THE GREAT DEFORMATION

An expanding federal government is a threat to our freedom. An expanding federal government and a shrinking economy are the biggest threats to our future. According to Congressional Budget Office projections, federal spending will increase as a percentage of GDP well into the future. Meanwhile, quantitative easing and low interest rates have benefitted the wealthy to the detriment of the middle class. So far, most newly created money has not penetrated the general economy where it would have helped most people. The word deformation means a change for the worse. David Stockman is the author of *The Great Deformation – The Corruption of Capitalism in America*, Public Affairs, 2013. Stockman believes America has slipped into crony capitalism, a symbiotic relationship between big business and the federal government.

FREEDOM FORCE INTERNATIONAL

According to G. Edward Griffin, Freedom Force International is a network of men and women from all parts of the world and all walks of life who are concerned over the loss of personal liberty and growth of government power ... in short, the mission of Freedom Force is nothing less than to be Guardians of liberty."

A minority of the population has always spearheaded political movements. In the American Revolution, there were two groups, one loyal to England and the other dedicated to America, while daily life consumed most people. Both the Globalists and Nationalists are small groups. Whichever wins this battle will earn the following of most people. Freedom Force International

CHAPTER 12: DEPRESSIONS

exposes the New World Order and educates people of its intentions of world domination. The Freedom Force educates, inspires, and admonishes citizens to preserve American values, policies, and laws. As Milton Friedman would often say, *"Freedom is not free."* Griffin states that for citizens of the world to attain prosperity and happiness, we, meaning people of the world, must reach for power—we must be forceful to win our freedom— thus the title Freedom Force International.

Freedom Force International has a YouTube site named Reality Zone. Reality Zone is a marketplace for books, audio, and videos dealing with freedom, health, and monetary issues. It is a marketing arm of American media; both companies are creations of G. Edward Griffin. The guiding theme of Freedom Force International is that it takes power to defend freedom. Suppose we the people cannot influence the political process, the corporate dominance over the news media. In that case, we leave the door open for world leaders to become tyrants. Our forefathers established this nation on the principle that the state must be limited to the defense of life, liberty, and property, and nothing more.

CONCLUSION

We face dangerous times as two opposing worlds collide. What is at stake is the sovereignty of nations, whether countries control their destiny or not. For a nation to be sovereign, to break free from the Globalists' power and all its branches—it must have control over its money supply and military. As long as a country has a stable and independent currency with value and a loyal army, the country can remain free and independent. But, if society accepts a digital currency that the government and banks

CHAPTER 12: DEPRESSIONS

control, then we lose our sovereignty, especially if a world bank controls the currency. Likewise, if a country melds its military into a global police force, like the United Nations Peace Keeping Force, national sovereignty is lost. What lies ahead will depend on which 3 percent of active people will win the general population's support.

The most pressing economic problem we face is excessive debt, especially for medium and small businesses. The debt load for the average family has increased substantially in the past generations. This increase in debt will usher in an economic collapse. Once the economy heads south, as it always does, consumers will not only spend less, but they will not be able to pay for the things already purchased, setting off a chain of events causing more unemployment. In addition, the excessive inventory will force businesses to cut back production and lay off workers. The only solution to this problem is a massive debt forgiveness program to alleviate the pressure on the middle class. If this does not happen, a significant economic collapse will wipe out all debt.

ABOUT THE AUTHOR

I grew up in the golden age of rock'n'roll; the fifties was a decade when music changed from being parent-friendly to teenagers going wild over Elvis Presley, Chuck Berry, and Jerry Lee Lewis. I started college in 1963, the year the Beatles appeared on the Ed Sullivan Show. I remember lying in bed and listening to songs like "Let it Be," "Help," and "A Hard Day's Night."

Then there was that sobering moment sitting in the bleachers at Eastern Michigan University and hearing that Lee Harvey Oswald had assassinated John F. Kennedy. Looking back, I can see that events were taking us from traditions of baseball, apple pie, and family dinners together, to a world that has grown darker.

Moving from Michigan with my wife, Kay, I was hired to teach economics at New River Community College in Dublin Virginia, which I am still doing 45 years later. I have written four books before this one. This book is the result of the painful process I had to fight through the propaganda, the disinformation, false teachings, half-truths, and groupthink. Knowledge is power, but the mainline news media lacks truth, and therefore the average person lacks power. My search led me to the alternative news media where I found well informed, truth-seeking, patriotic people.

Find out more about Ken at: kennethelongauthor.com

www.ingramcontent.com/pod-product-compliance
Lightning Source LLC
Chambersburg PA
CBHW071459040426
42444CB00008B/1404